Priest and Worker

Priest and Worker

The Autobiography of Henri Perrin

**Translated and with an
Introduction by Bernard Wall**

New York   Chicago   San Francisco
Holt, Rinehart and Winston

NIHIL OBSTAT
Brendan Lawlor
Censor Deputatus

IMPRIMATUR
✠ Robert F. Joyce
Bishop of Burlington, Vt.
March 31, 1964

The nihil obstat and imprimatur are official declarations that a book or pamphlet is free of doctrinal or moral error. No implication is contained therein that those who have granted the nihil obstat and imprimatur agree with the contents, opinions, or statements expressed.

First Edition

Designer: Ernst Reichl

86998–0114

Printed in the United States of America

Contents

Priest and Worker

INTRODUCTION

The Drama of the Priest-Workers

HENRI PERRIN, whose tragic story of suffering and disillusionment is told in this book assembled by his friends, was a typical priest-worker.

Although his story can be understood only against the background of French politics and religion, it also has a universal bearing as part of a struggle to find a meeting-ground between what is considered essential in the Christian mission and the intellectual and practical demands of modern life. In no country have so many attempts been made in this direction as in France. On the intellectual plane, with *The Phenomenon of Man*, Teilhard de Chardin attempted to reconcile Christianity with evolutionary cosmology and biology. On the practical side, the priest-workers were attempting to bridge the gap between religion and the mass of the proletariat, to whom the very idea of a priest was an anachronism or the subject of tired jokes about celibacy. Both these attempts ran into difficulties in Rome, where the

3

weight of two thousand years of history and habit seemed to be overwhelmingly against experiment.

The priest-worker movement was an immediate outcome of World War II, but it would scarcely have been possible without events that had occurred much earlier.

There has, in fact, been something like a civil war in France ever since the Revolution in 1789. It has been a war of ideas between Right and Left; although only occasionally flaring up into violence, it has split the country in two. In the early stages, on one side were the old aristocracy and their followers, who have always been far more numerous and intelligent than people outside France imagine. On the other side were the middle classes and the liberal intelligentsia. In time a new pattern emerged. The spokesmen of the Church, who were overwhelmingly right wing, favored the property owners and the rich in general, although they would never have admitted it in those terms; the farmers and peasants—especially in regions such as Brittany and Alsace—clung to the Church. But the industrial workers abandoned it; to them it seemed that the Church was involved in class war, and on the opposite side.

Something rather similar happened in eighteenth-century England during the Industrial Revolution. The Church of England, which was the official religion of the State, was supported by the squires and the peasants. But the working classes fell away from it, feeling that this "ruling-class religion" had no message for them. The man who saw that England was being divided into "two nations"—the prosperous who kept the outward observances of the Church, and the poor who were not at home in the Church—was John Wesley. In France there was no one like Wesley, with his mission to the masses, until the advent of the priest-workers.

The movement began during the German occupation of France in World War II. Numbers of young priests—Henri Perrin was one of them—joined the battalions of workers conscripted into German industry. About the same time (1943), Cardinal Suhard, Archbishop of Paris, asked two young priests to prepare a report on the relationship between the Church and the working classes in France. The report, which appeared in book form as *France, Pays de Mission,** became the handbook of enthusiastic young priests and caused something of a sensation throughout the country. The essential thesis of *France, Pays de Mission* was that it was absolutely pointless for churchmen to go on behaving in their traditional way, saying Mass in their cold and empty churches for a few middle-aged spinsters and reluctant altar boys, when the vast majority of Frenchmen, and especially the industrial workers, had lost contact with the Church altogether and could only be approached in a "missionary" spirit (like the "pagans" of Africa) with a technique adapted to their special circumstances. In 1944, the "Mission de Paris" (the mission to the working classes in the Paris area) was set up, and various dioceses in the provinces, such as Lyons and Marseilles, followed suit. Young seminarians studying to become the new missionaries spent part of their time in factories and workshops, and young priests began doing full shifts in the factories, sharing the lot of their fellows. The only difference between their circumstances and those of the other workers was that they were unmarried and said Mass.

• This book, adapted into English by Maisie Ward, appeared under the title *France, Pagan?* (New York: Sheed & Ward, Inc., 1949)

The movement attracted ardent young men full of zeal for "winning the world for Christ," in a way the routine life of the ordinary parish could never attract them. It was also supported by members of the religious orders—to some extent the Jesuits, whom Perrin joined, but above all, the Dominicans; the latter controlled or inspired such influential periodicals as *La Vie Intellectuelle, La Vie Spirituelle,* and *Actualité Religieuse dans le Monde* (continued as *Informations catholique internationales*). These periodicals were edited in the avant-garde spirit which was expressed by such philosophers and writers as Jacques Maritain, who combined orthodox Thomist interpretations in metaphysical matters with advanced social views, and François Mauriac, the novelist and political commentator. One of the Dominicans, Père Montuclard, took a more extreme position in the journal, *Jeunesse de l'église.* "The leading idea of this group, expressed in a regular series of booklets, was that we are living in a period between two eras of history. This is an age of transition and of waiting, the 'age of John the Baptist.' The role of the Church and of the apostles is to help the change at the temporal level, in effect to support the proletarian revolution and await the crystallization of a new civilization before attempting the work of evangelization. . . ."•

This extreme view, which was eventually condemned by the French bishops as well as by Rome, undoubtedly represented one tendency among the priest-workers themselves. It provided the conservatives with ammunition. But the fact was that the priest-workers were regarded with suspicion in clerically oriented circles, not by the French clergy as such, nor by many of the bishops and archbishops, but by

• John Fitsimons, *Blackfriars,* February, 1954.

all the static forces: businessmen, industrialists, and the rich middle classes who had been brought up to think of the Church as their ally who would always defend the rights of property. In addition to using their influence with the press and the French Church to eliminate the priest-workers, these people even lobbied in Rome itself.

The nature of the argument and the agony of conscience that it caused are written in blood in this book. The problem was more or less as follows.

If the priest-workers were to become genuine workers and not mere propaganda squads playing a game, they had to live in tenements or slums with other workers, enduring all the discomforts and ill-health that might go with this way of life. But more than this. It was not possible for them to be genuine workers without becoming members of a *syndi- cat*, or trade union. In France, trade union life plays an even more important part than in the English-speaking countries. There is something amounting almost to a mystique about the working classes, and they have a mutual solidarity pos- sibly unique in Western countries.

The real difficulty arose from the fact that the largest of all the trade unions in France, the C.G.T. (Confédération Générale de Travail), is more or less dominated by the Communist Party. This means not only that it struggles for an improved standard of living for the workers, with the ultimate aim of destroying the whole capitalist system, but also that it operates *politically* on occasion, as a sort of in- direct organ of the Soviet foreign office and of Russian power politics. The Communist Party is obliged to justify all Soviet activities—even when these include shooting down the working classes, as in East Germany and Hungary. Because of their superior education and their volunteer enthusiasm, the priest-workers rapidly distinguished themselves among their fellow workers and rose to positions of responsibility and authority in the unions; Henri Perrin, for example, became secretary of his union at the Isère-Arc works. Yet in 1949 the Holy Office in Rome had excommunicated not only all members of the Communist Party, but also anyone who assisted Communists or associated with them. The priest-workers were thus involved in a peculiar paradox of modern times. All modern socialist and reformist movements for the easing of man's lot stem from Christianity, in the sense that they would be unthinkable had there been no Christianity in history. The working-class leaders were more Christian than they knew, although they denied affiliation with any creed. The Communist Party itself can be understood to have Christian origins, but unfortunately has become a dogmatic antichurch.

From 1949 on, the priest-workers were aware of the cloud on the horizon; the machinery had been mounted by the Holy Office that would ultimately lead to their condemnation. Inevitably, if they were members of the C.G.T., they consorted with Communists, yet if they resigned from the C.G.T. and abandoned all union activity, they would be viewed as traitors to the working classes and would have to face the reproach that Henri Perrin dreaded so much: "We always knew priests could never be on the side of the workers. We trusted you, and now look what has happened."

What saved the movement for the time being from the disapproval of Rome—and of such prominent figures in the Curia as Cardinal Ottaviani—was the French bishops. While disapproving of extremists such as Père Montuclard, the French hierarchy wished to preserve the essence of the new missionary fervor. Tension between the French Church and the Vatican increased, and there was deep resentment among many French Catholics at what seemed one further example of reactionary interference from Rome.

The story of how the priest-worker experiment was stopped is told in this book, but it is worth while recapitulating the events. In 1953 the group of priest-workers operating from Paris was told to take no further recruits. Then Cardinal Pizzardo, of the Roman Curia, and Prefect of the Congregation of Seminaries, wrote a letter to the archbishops and bishops in France forbidding seminarians to work for short periods in mines or factories. At the end of the year Cardinals Liénart, Gerlier, and Feltin went to Rome to try to reach some sort of agreement with the Holy See, and returned with an arrangement that appeared to be a compromise between the Roman view and their own. Priest-workers were to live henceforth in a presbytery or at least in a community of priests. They were to do only part-time work in factories and should retire from all activity in the unions.

These terms were a complete rejection of what Henri Perrin and others like him had dreamed of—that their movement would spread among priests and that "even a bishop" should take up factory work so as to see for himself what the conditions of the working classes really were. An appalling crisis of conscience began. Several scores of priests felt that they could not abandon the positions of trust they occupied in the ranks of the workers, and preferred to face ecclesiastical ban and excommunication rather than do so. If they could no longer operate as priests, they could at least continue as workers and await the day when different policies prevailed in Rome. The French bishops by and large showed understanding and humanity to the men of this stricken movement. They tried to soft-pedal the fierce Roman demands and, not surprisingly, felt indignation at the way Rome had gone over their heads.

The disagreement with Rome led to a crisis in the French Dominican Order, which had been in the forefront of the defense of the priest-workers. By 1954, rumors were circulating to the effect that Rome intended to dissolve the Order in France. To avoid this extreme development, the General of the Order sought a compromise and dismissed the Provincials of Paris, Toulouse, and Lyons from office. In addition, four of the best-known Dominicans in Paris were reduced to silence—Père Chenu, a medievalist and professor at the Collège de France, who was theological adviser to the Young Christian Workers and the priest-workers; Père Féret, professor at the Institut Catholique in Paris; Père Boisselot, director of the Dominican publishing house, Les Editions du Cerf, and editor of *Actualité Religieuse dans le Monde*; and Père Congar. Further, it was decreed that all books written by the French Dominicans would be subject to a special censorship by the Holy Office.

We must remember that the priest-worker experiment took place in the forties and the early fifties, at a time when France was still recovering from the effects of World War II. The wretched lot of the French industrial workers, their low pay and miserable housing conditions—which incited Henri Perrin and his colleagues to indignation and action—have now been considerably alleviated. Naturally, no wages in European countries can be compared with those in the United States, but by and large the French worker lives as well as any other worker in Western Europe. As everywhere else, whole categories of skilled workers in France tend to think more and more in terms of the installments to be paid on the car, the refrigerator, and the washing machine, and where to spend the summer holidays next year. The share the workers now enjoy in the general prosperity of their country was certainly increased by the union activity in which the priest-workers thought it a privilege to participate. But their attempt to "spiritualize" such action has left few visible results. In a sense this attempt was grotesquely ambitious in relation to the means at their disposal. For there were never more than two hundred priest-workers, whereas the unions numbered their supporters by the million. The priest-workers were aware of this, but they thought they were starting a new era in the history of Christianity and that the idea would spread to other European countries where the dissociation between the Church and the working classes has considerable similarity to the French situation.

The reasons given in Rome for the suppression of the priest-workers had some basis in fact. There is no doubt that in their enthusiasm for the working classes they became involved in political activities, and they often leaned nearer to Communism than they knew. But the basic question they raised about the nature and destiny of Christianity has never really been answered. Inevitably, after two thousand years of incorporation into Western history, Christianity is in one aspect a conservative establishment. Can it remain such? Periodically, there have been efforts to apply the Sermon on the Mount to practical life, but the paths of reformers have rarely been easy.

Henri Perrin frequently said that Christianity should leave

the "ghetto," should cease to be a "sect" on the defensive, and that the Christian priest should go out into "the world" fearlessly as a "man among men." This emphasis on being a "man" was a result of the fact that popular opinion in France tends to view priests as a third sex—as creatures who are neither men nor women. In Perrin's view, as in that of other priest-workers, it was only in overalls that the priest could speak to other workers as an equal. He would never be accepted by the masses as long as he trailed about in a long black soutane, preached about things that, rightly or wrongly, were meaningless to his contemporaries, contentedly repeated pious platitudes, and trained a choir to sing sugary hymns that had no connection with the taste of the age. Henri Perrin wished to abolish, not what he considered the essential mission of the priesthood, but the two thousand years of accretions that had accumulated around this mission. In theory, there might seem to be a clear distinction between the essence and the accretions, but practice is another matter.

As regards Communism and "the world," the attitude taken in Rome seems in great part to have been dictated by fear and something like a feeling of inferiority. Was it taken for granted that if a priest met a Communist, he would be converted by the Communist rather than convert him? And if so, why? Were priests safe only if they were separated from other men in their "ghetto"? Whatever the answers, certainly this was the interpretation of the process by which the priest-worker movement was suppressed.

It might have been argued by the ecclesiastical authorities that the activism necessary to industrial life is opposed to the spirit of contemplation and tranquillity that religions from

Christianity to Buddhism teach. There is a genuine problem here, and plainly Perrin found it difficult to combine contemplation and prayer with being a strike leader. The lot of the factory worker in any society, whether ours or the Russian, may seem a desperate one, on the human even more than on the economic level, but society being what it is, how can the less privileged escape this lot? As long as we demand the benefits of industrial production, there have to be factory workers. The priest-workers at least brought a sense of the sacred into a world in which reminders of God had been all but obliterated.

As things were, the spirit of the condemnation seemed hardly the spirit of pioneers; and if a negative attitude had been the Church's rule from the beginning, it is hard to see quite how the Christian impetus would have gathered force.

Yet the suffering of Henri Perrin and of other priest-workers was not uncreative. They made no mean contribution to the change of spirit which, with the reign of Pope John XXIII and Vatican Council II, was about to animate the headquarters of the faith itself. It is too early to say how long the principle of *aggiornamento*, "bringing up to date," announced by Pope John, will take to penetrate down to the roots of etiquette, tradition, and legalism to which the Roman Curia has been committed. But no one who reads Pope John's writings or considers the acts of the first session of his Council can doubt the existence of the wind of change. Pope Paul VI, with the second session of the Council, has committed himself to carrying on Pope John's work. It seems as if the whole world has been waiting for a spiritual lead from Rome, and the new initiative has been welcomed by men and women of every belief—Orthodox, Protestants, Hindus, agnostics, humanists, and Communists. The conception that all men, regardless of creed, are brothers is rooted in the Gospels themselves, and on our precarious earth the change of attitude in the Church of Rome has already given new hope and encouragement to all mankind.

Bernard Wall

London, 1963

I

Early Years

(1914–1942)

Henri Perrin was born on April 13, 1914, at Cornimont, not far from Gerardmer, in a valley high up in the Vosges Mountains, whose opposite slope overlooks the plain of Alsace. The fir-covered peaks that dominate the quiet little village of Cornimont have been a frontier, between wars, and a front, during wars. When the Germans retreated in 1944 it was here that they made a stand for a month or two, devastating the forests and villages round about.

Henri was only two when his father was killed at Noulette, near Lorette, in World War I. For months he was reported missing, and it was not until Henri was seventeen that he discovered his father's grave at Lorette.

Henri's grandmother, mother, and sister Andrée, like most of the women in the Hautes Vosges, went to work in the textile mills. The knowledge and acceptance of poverty came easily to Henri, and although his childhood may have been

clouded by the absence of a father, he was on the whole a
healthy and happy child.

In 1926 he entered the seminary at Mattaincourt. Nowa-
days it seems extraordinary to enter a seminary at the age of
twelve, but at that time it was quite common. It was not a
system that always worked well, and many of the boys later
left. Henri, although an outdoor boy and not good at studies,
began to develop deep religious interests, and he managed
to get through the baccalaureate in 1930.

The decade from 1930 to 1940 was one of intense activity
in French Catholicism, and this ferment was reflected in
seminaries and novice houses. The Jeunesse Ouvrière Chré-
tienne, or Young Christian Workers (that "Pentecostal
flame," as Mauriac called it) had recently been founded by
Canon Cardijn in Belgium; Emmanuel Mounier was planning and launching *Esprit,* an international journal reflect-
ing the Catholic personalism of its founder, and providing
a forum for like-minded Christians, Jews, socialists, and agnostics who wished to attack the "established disorder." The
Dominicans launched *La Vie Intellectuelle,* to be followed
shortly by the weekly, *Sept.* All these periodicals were deeply
involved in the social problem from an advanced Christian
point of view, and had their influence in what became
known as the "Age of the Popular Front." Henri witnessed
and shared in this deep thirst for spiritual and social renewal.
Both at the seminary and during holidays, he kept up a lively
correspondence with friends who shared his preoccupations,
but most of this correspondence is now lost. Intermittently
he kept a diary. In 1933 he began confiding in a Jesuit priest
at Nancy. Here are a few extracts from his notebooks and
letters:

During the last three months I have been able to resolve all my difficulties before nightfall in front of the crucifix or tabernacle. This life is easy in a way, and yet how much it demands from one! (February 7, 1936)

Though the atmosphere in a seminary can be oppressive, work is at all times possible—and quite a different kind of work from learning to teach the catechism or plan study circles and holiday camps. (May 31, 1937)

For some time I have been wondering seriously about the extent to which we can estimate the value of our own effort. We know very little about the progress of the divine life within us. When are we gaining, and when losing? Only the Holy Spirit really knows.

His ideas developed further after a visit to Africa, which was the outcome of his energetic propaganda for the weekly, *Sept.*

Do you know what idea I'm keenest on now? It's that we still have a lot of work to do together, helping one another, in order to develop something resembling a Christian mentality. This, and acquiring a Christian temperament, will take years and years of work. And it will need heroism. I keep thinking of this because we have second-rate bourgeois values all around us, tempting us; there is everything to encourage us to accept a comfortable place in a corrupt civilization. (September 2, 1935)

I think I have discarded some of the prejudices imposed on us for so long by our environment, education, and traditions. Veritas liberabit vos. We are surrounded by so many false conventions, selfish motives, and other forms of narrowness. It's appalling. René, you ask for indulgence toward the clergy. For their personalities, all right. But for their habits, their let-things-be mentality, no; we have to be extremely severe with ourselves. (September 19, 1936)

In the eyes of the world, including the clerical world, which has lost every notion of integral Christianity, a real priest must look like a madman. That's what's so terrifying —the need to make renunciations that so many others don't make, don't even dream of. Will I be brave enough? (May 21, 1937)

Henri Perrin spent a good deal of time at this period in social work. There were the Semaines Sociales—study gatherings for social questions—and there was Catholic Action in the J.O.C. (Young Christian Workers) and the J.A.C. (Young Christian Agricultural Workers). He visited factories in Lille, and organized holiday camps. He spent his two years of military service (October, 1935 to September, 1937) in Beirut, where he was assigned to the University. He describes his teaching experience with enthusiasm:

One of the things that most impelled me not to let my eyes leave that ideal of living with the Lord was the class of boys that was entrusted to me: twenty-six fifth-formers. We set out together in search of Christ, our Brother. We wanted to live with Him, and were caught in a trap from which there was no escape.

We got to know this Brother a little better. While studying prayer, we composed a class prayer, the only real prayer *that was possible. Each boy made up his own version, and I brought together the best suggestions in a single prayer. This was tacked up on the wall, along with the picture from the Jocist calendar (the young worker bearing his burden and offering his hand to Christ, who is carrying the cross).*

We were then led to decide on a daily moment of meditation, and for two months we were faithful to it.

A large map of Europe was specially drawn up, and different groups did reports on the worst areas of poverty and the great needs of the world.

And all the other things—the class mite box, the class library, decorating the classroom, going to the movies or on hikes, singing—we began to do more and more together. And all this in order to live, joyously, in Christ, together. (February 7, 1936)

Henri must have been an attractive teacher for young boys. Slim and of medium height, he had an open and rather long face. He always gave the impression that he was younger than he really was, but his friends all describe him as the natural leader in any group or team.

While at Beirut he was able to make a visit to the Holy Land. Before returning to the seminary for his last year of preparation for the priesthood, he had two months of travel in Egypt, Greece, Turkey, Bulgaria, Roumania, Yugoslavia, and Germany.

On October 9, 1938, he was ordained priest at Saint-Die. After his ordination, Henri Perrin was attached to the Institut Catholique in Paris and at last had the opportunity of coming into contact with the intellectual life and social work of the capital. But this period was short-lived, for in September, 1939, war broke out and he was called up in an Algerian regiment. Eight months later he was captured at Sedan, and during the French collapse was selected to nurse the wounded at the hospital at Commercy. For his war activities he was awarded the Croix de Guerre. Demobilized, he decided against remaining an ordinary secular priest, and applied to enter the Jesuit novitiate, which had been evacuated to Cazières-sur-Adour in the Landes. There is substantial documentation about his life at this period in letters written to a cousin who had become a Carmelite nun:

I have been thinking of you constantly and fully believe that you have never missed a day praying for me. . . . You wonder how my year's novitiate has gone? The main thing about it seems to have been the calm. No great difficulties. God hasn't asked me for more than a loving acceptance of the little nothings that fill a novice's day, a spirit of mortification in small matters, and the renunciation of my will in tiny details. I still have the same idea—of reaching the point when I shall live in the intimate presence of Christ. But I have learned that the real way of doing this is by the prayer and mortification required by the Rule. And what I think I've really gained this year is a solid basis for my spiritual life, an armor and principles it previously lacked. My spiritual life seems better organized, rather than enriched, and that was just what was needed.

We carried out the thirty days' Exercises of Saint Ignatius —almost all of them, except for night meditation. It's incredible—a real bath of silence, recollection, and intense life with God. After that, the months passed by in prayer, study of the Rule, a little general study, and work in the fields. If you include reciting the breviary and saying Mass, I've been spending six hours a day praying. So you see the

sort of food we live on. Because of present conditions I've
had to officiate a bit in neighboring villages, but that hasn't
upset my life as a novice. This evening we're entering the end
of the year's retreat, and I'm going to weigh the pros and cons
of my progress. I shall be counting on your prayers more than
ever.

I must stop for a while. I've got to go and say Mass at two
neighboring parishes. The Masses are very late, at eleven and
twelve. Off I go. I'll be remembering you at the altar. Till
this evening. . . .

Here I am back again. As I promised, I didn't forget you.
I'll remember you even more than usual this week, which I
want to devote to intense recollection. I'm counting on you,
and rely on your prayers more than ever. . . .

Between Cazières-sur-Adour and the College of Montgré,
October 15, 1941 (Feast of St. Theresa of Avila)

I'm writing this from Tarbes. I left the novitiate at midday today. As you can guess, I've been spending the day with
you in corde Christi. It's exactly a year since I entered the
religious order and put myself in the hands of Saint Theresa.
My canonical year ends today. Now more than ever I shall
count on you and my Trappist brother. As I'm already an
ordained priest, I have only one year's novitiate instead of
two. I'll be doing another year (the famous tertianship) in
seven or eight years' time, when my studies are completed.
Till then we are bound only by simple, but perpetual, vows;
but after tertianship, if we are accepted, we make solemn
vows.

For the present, it is a life of study, a life that has to be
impregnated with contemplation and prayer. I have set my
ideal high, as you asked me to. Christ expects a lot; help me

not to disappoint Him too much. You must be wondering what this ideal is that I'm taking along as I leave the novitiate. Don't worry, it's the one I told you about fifteen months ago, that I've been holding to for the last ten years —but now it has been renewed, deepened and enriched: to live Christ, Jesus present and loved, everywhere and in all things.

To get down to details. Here are a few notes on the essential gains of my year's novitiate. To begin with, the discovery of how weak and poor I am, as well as another benefit that is a normal result of entry into the life of a religious: straightening out the question of mortification (both interior and exterior). This had been bothering me for a long time, and it's rarely referred to by the secular clergy. Wanting the cross, and loving it—at least a beginning in this direction. One thing that isn't restricted to the Jesuits, but which St. Ignatius sets at the very heart of the spiritual life and makes a rule for his followers, is the will to imitate Jesus in his suffering, out of love for Him, the desire for the cross and suffering and humiliation so as to become more like Our Lord.

Along with the idea of the glory of God and the call of the kingdom, this seems to me one of the peaks—and also one of the foundations—of Jesuit spirituality. But this spirituality of constant and close union with Christ in the deepest humility and generosity, the thing you find on every page of the Constitutions and in every Rule—this is by no means my only discovery. There is still the matter of living these things. Help me. . . .

Next: future plans. I'm going to Lyons to meet Mother and all Andrée's little family. We'll be talking about you, need I say. Then on to the Montgré College, near Lyons,

where I'm to spend a year studying literature for my degree.
. . . Let's pray together for ourselves and the world. I'm
counting very much on you and would like to pay you back as
best I can. With great thanks, in Our Lady and in corde
Christi.

A year later, after his first twelve months at Lyons, he
wrote to his Carmelite cousin:

Montgré, October 10, 1942
I have spent my year studying: two exams in July (one
failed) and two within a week from now. Then I go to Puy
for a year's philosophy. A bit of parish work has enabled me
to maintain direct contact with souls, especially during the
holidays when I was parish priest, and for a while as chaplain
to some scouts. This last job gave me the wonderful privilege
of joining the Puy pilgrimage on August 15 and of praying
there with all those fine young people.

Vals, November 9, 1942
My dear Sister. You must have been expecting a long
newsy letter from me for ages. I hope you got my postcard
a few weeks ago and are awaiting the happy day. Here it is
at last. The Society has accepted me as a member, and on the
21st of this month I'll be making my private perpetual vow
of poverty, chastity, and obedience. And you can imagine
the great joy it will give me to know that on that day I will
have not only Mother and my Superiors near me, before
God our Father, but also the invisible presence of my Carmelite sister and my Trappist brother, with whom I have
vowed to work side by side in our Father's field; both you and
he, who have gone before me into the religious life, will pre-

sent me to our Master as another you, as one who should be
the fulfillment of your apostolic desires, as the humanity
through whom you will act upon souls.

As I told you, I was prevented from writing to you only
by the demands of work this year and the endless pages of
Greek, for our communion is stronger, deeper, and more
active than ever, rest assured of that. Just as I see my life as
a priest and a religious only as a complete dedication to the
work of the redemption and the return of our fellow men
to their Father, so your presence near me seems the necessary and solid foundation of a life totally given over to the
apostolate. As I am always saying, I count on you and you are
necessary to me; it is side by side and by God's will that we
are saving the world; and this collaboration of ours will become even closer in a few days when our lives will be bound
by the same vows. Our collaboration will last until we are
presented with the laus perennis in heaven. But by then we
must have around us and perhaps ahead of us—in the love
of the Father and in the heart of our Christ—a crowd of
souls to whom we shall have given life and joy. Laetatus sum
in his quae dicta sunt mihi; in domum Domini ibimus.
. . . O what joy!

I am entering the religious life with various ideas I want
to tell you about, because they'll help you to imagine better
the work in which you are collaborating. As I've told you before, the central idea of my life in the last ten years has been
God's presence in us by way of grace and fidelity to his love.
The last two years of preparation have anchored me still
further in this idea of God's presence, the astounding life
of charity, constant wonder at the thought that we are his
sons, his Son, and how we live a family life with Him—
domestici Dei—and that He loves us as his children. I have

never grasped this so well as during this last year, and I feel
I'll never understand it, it's so utterly amazing. As a result,
I want to strive with all my power never to lose this presence,
to live by it, to nourish myself on it, to strengthen myself
with it, and to live a life worthy of it. How I have delighted
in St. Bernard's fine saying this year: Undique inhaerent
Deus et homo, undique inhaerent perpetua et intima dilectione, tamquam inviscerati alterutrum sibi.* It's untrans-
latable! Forgive me. I found huge joy in discovering the same
idea at every moment in the Constitutions of St. Ignatius:
men united with God, men finding God in all things; that's
the one and only thing He asks for. I also found it in a book
you may know, the eighteenth-century Fondements de la
Vie spirituelle by Fr. Surin.

But perhaps what makes an even deeper mark on me is the
revelation of our union with everyone in Christ, the mystical
body, the Church, the social meaning of all Christian life,
the sacraments, the religious life, etc. Every moment I'm
making fresh discoveries in this area. I've had two meditations in the space of a month on the Epistle to the Ephesians,
and thought how far we still are from St. Paul's spirit! How
individualist our prayer is, how stunted our piety, how
cramped our religious life, and how shrunken our Masses, reduced to little individual devotional practices. And meanwhile the Christian people is dying and there's hardly anyone
left to proclaim the Father's burning love, hardly anyone
to give others the desire to be Christian, to create the con-
tagion of Christ. Of course you will realize I'm not the
only person worried by these questions; this is the whole

* God and man commingle at every point; they commingle by means of
an intimate and perpetual love, as though interlocked by limb and fiber
one with the other.

current of thinking today, the current of Catholic Action. I experienced it again on the Puy pilgrimage, and I think it's the thing that will save us. The latest book I've been reading along these lines is Father de Lubac's Catholicisme. Have you come across it?

I shall stop now, for I've told you the gist, and the rest can come some other time. This way you'll be able to accompany me in my work of self-formation, with a year of philosophy now, then theology next year, and the odd bits of parish work I'm carrying on at the moment—with a Young Christian Farmers' circle in a little village near here and weekly confessions in a nearby agricultural college. Entrust us to the care of Jeannette, to whom I am so devoted.* And for my part I entrust you, and the whole of Carmel that's praying for us, to the care of Our Lady of Puy.

* Joan of Arc, the saint of his native Lorraine.

II

The German Experience (1943–1944)

HENRI PERRIN passed the next stage of his life (1943–1944), a short but very full one, as a worker in Germany and as a clandestine chaplain among the French deportees.

Concern for prisoners first and foremost, and then for labor conscripts, was very lively in Christian circles in France. Thanks to the Aumonerie Générale des Prisonniers (General Chaplaincy for Prisoners), organized by the Abbé Rodhain, a tight network of material help had been established between parishes at home and camps in Germany. Priests who were prisoners were the natural intermediaries in this campaign. Sustained not only by food but also by books and liturgical nourishment, important cells of Catholic Action came into being, inspired by the youth movements of the 1930–1940 period.

But when the Germans began conscripting French civilians for forced labor in Germany, a fresh problem arose. There could be no chaplains, for the Germans would not

allow priests in. The result was that numbers of priests
volunteered to go to Germany *as workers*. One of the first
accepted was Henri Perrin. However, after spending a short
time near Leipzig, he was discovered to be a priest, was
arrested, imprisoned, and subsequently sent back to France.
The majority of his colleagues, when exposed, ended up in
concentration camps.

During this period Henri Perrin kept a journal of his
experiences.* We can follow his life through extracts from
this journal and from correspondence. He was now twenty-
eight.

To his Carmelite cousin:

Leipzig, October 29, 1943
*My dearest Sister. I've just received, through Mother, a
copy of your letter and Sister Elizabeth's prayer, as well as
the music score. Everything was opened by the censor, who
made a careful note on the letter to the effect that it was
accompanied by a holy picture and a song. The holy picture
was crossed by two brush marks, one red and one blue. I'll
treasure it all the more. I treasure everything in this little
packet—I've been searching for the complete text of Sister
Elizabeth's prayer for four years. You can count on its providing food for my own prayers during my hours of work.
And thanks, too, for the quotation from St. Ignatius that you
wrote at the bottom; I haven't overlooked that either. . . .
Christ is being very good to me, and his presence imposes
itself upon me, without my seeking it, the moment that I'm
alone. You can imagine how it animates my twelve hours'*

* Subsequently published in English as *Priest-Workman in Germany*
(New York: Sheed & Ward, Inc., 1947).

night shift. For at the moment I'm having the joy of keeping watch, like you, and even more than you, for I don't get to bed before eight in the morning. More than once I've joined you in spirit when saying Compline at about ten at night, or at the Deus, ad Te de luce vigilo at Lauds at two in the morning. Did you know that the first Masses I've been able to say here have been at a Carmelite convent? And then a friend has brought me a copy of Études Carmélitaines, on "the Christian risk," which I'm going to read—and that will be yet another link with you. A stage toward the perfect communion that will come someday between us and Him. So there you are. Mother will have given you other news from me. All is going very well. Someday I'll tell you about it all at length. . . .

Excerpts from Henri Perrin's journal as a priest-worker in Germany:

Saturday, October 30, 1943

Again on my way south, where thirty seminarians are expecting me. Going along in the train, the memories of my major seminary came and went. What would I have done had I been sent to Germany ten years sooner?

In France, everyone was very concerned with adapting young priests to their new way of life [in Germany]. But in fact, wherever I go, I can tell, merely by talking to the priests, that things aren't what they should be; they are lacking in so many things—spirituality, apostleship, adaptability to material conditions. Mere impressions, too fragmentary to generalize upon, but too distinct and too serious to be taken lightly; and I note them down all the more freely because I feel deeply that I am one of these.

Here they are, witnesses of Christ, whom one would wish
to radiate his strength and his peace. One would wish them
in the thick of the fight, happy to carry Him among the
pagan masses: on the watch for souls needing protection or
care. They should be facing life proudly, overflowing with
the love which they alone possess, standing above the world
from the height of Christ, "volunteers" of the kingdom, in
love with the unique adventure in which God has involved
them. In this life to which they are bound we would want
them not merely to be free, but full of initiative, going forward on the offensive, outstripping others and drawing them
after them.

In fact they give the impression of young men who once
undoubtedly had enthusiasm and dreamed seriously of
conquering the world, but now they have been tamed, so
that their fire, if not extinguished, has become a night light.
They seem to hesitate and falter when faced with life, to
draw back from it almost timidly, as if they should ask
pardon from those around them for being Christians. A lot
of them grumble at having had to come here at all and, re-
signing themselves to the ordeal, fall little by little into
bitterness and resentment. They show a sort of weakness, an
inferiority complex—even toward Catholic Action militants.
They don't see themselves as doing compulsory service for
Christ; their lives aren't guided by their ideal; their faith
doesn't seem to channel off the best in them; their youthful
need for danger and heroism finds an outlet in the perform-
ance merely of material sabotage; their interior life seems
joyless and unproductive; and their too frequent physical
failings make it even worse. Often, spirituality means simply
holding on to certain pious practices—"my" prayers, "my"
interior life—and leads to a tendency to cut themselves off,

to be always on the defensive against their environment, to huddle together. You would think they have nothing to offer the world dying before their eyes, as if they're beaten and crushed by the life seething round them.

End of November, 1943

In launching the Groupe d'Amitié, my first intention was to "hook" the men by forming groups, seeing this as merely a way—a trick, if you like—of making contact with them, more or less forcing them to listen to me, and then posing the religious question to any who proved receptive. All our services were set up chiefly as a means of penetrating, so as to gain influence and make it easier to reach individual souls. A second aim was to camouflage the part of our activity that was strictly Catholic under a vast social activity, which was accepted and recognized by the Germans.

But more and more during these last weeks, it has seemed to me that our work ought to be not a conquest of individuals (whom we must at all costs "bring in," once they have been drawn to us) but a completely disinterested and free serving of the community. We should present to people the testimony of an attractive friendliness and utter generosity, but leave them totally free to find their way themselves to the God we love. We want to penetrate the institution and get hold of its inner workings—not to establish our influence there and do recruiting work, but to make things as much better as possible, to set up the community on Christian principles, believing with our whole soul that that is the only way to found a solid society built on happiness and love. That is why we can, and we must, stand openly for Christ and the Church. Others are absolutely free as far as we are concerned; nobody asks them to go to Mass or Confession; they must judge the tree by its fruit; and if their hearts are in the right place, they can follow us. Our friendship is there to help them, even to influence them, but God wants the adoration and love of free men.

Our attitude is becoming clearer on this point every day, and the results are not slow in coming. Above all, our fellow workers feel that "we believe in it," and the idea that we want to pester them with our "practices" hasn't crossed their minds. It's much better for them to find out in their own good time that these "practices" give us our life. More than one has already come and admitted that he envies us and that he, too, is in search of an ideal. Pierre, our camp sluggard, is waking up to the deeper meaning of life; Marcel, our young Belgian, is drawing nearer and nearer; a host of others find themselves, little by little, rising upward and looking for something better than they have; and when they talk to us we are able to explain to them how Mass and Communion are real food to us which, through us, becomes the food of others.

November 25, 1943

Presence of God. Sometimes, in the evenings, the universe becomes wonderfully near and homely. Everything is peaceful, linked together and filled with the visible presence of God.

On the stroke of eight o'clock the factory takes up its rhythm, which nothing will disturb till tomorrow morning. Our workshop is the only one with a night shift, and we're as peaceful as craftsmen in the lamplight.

It is then that I often go and sit outside on the red benches facing the setting sun. The plain of Saxony stretches as far as the horizon, without the smallest hill, and the sky is immensely pure and calm. A late bus may cross the Delitsch road, and then all is silence again. In the distance there's a light that hasn't yet been blacked-out; as night falls you feel the presence of a home, the beating heart of a family: a man, a woman, children, God.

Against the horizon, a forest, an incarnation of the Heimat, rests and keeps watch. A light shoots up on the far left; the searchlight has cast its beam far up and slowly explores the sky; then others light up on the right, in the middle—four, five, sometimes ten—their rays meeting and crossing in majestic silence.

From behind me, dulled by the closed doors, comes the faint whirring of machines. It's like a background accompaniment, over which one's mind can weave what it likes. Sometimes I feel lost in wonder before the strength of the machines (just try to stop a cylinder or a mandrel, however slowly it's going!), this enormous strength, gentle and brutal, so docile to those who know how to handle it, that thumps, rends, penetrates, bores, glazes, smooths, polishes. And all around us, there are the workers, who make up another universe. Whoever they are, they have their own personal gestures at times: a glance, a movement, an attitude, a smile, a way of leaning over the machine, of feeling the tool edge, of taking a piece of bread, of telling me about their kids— those little refinements that come near to being a prayer. They have no idea how much I love them; and when I leave them in the chill of dawn, my head throbbing and my fingers trembling with the fatigue of the night, and lift up the Host at Mass, they don't know how heavily my hands are weighted with their whole life, with all their suffering of the night, which I long to charge with love as one charges an electric battery.

They don't know, and have no means of knowing, because they don't know God. They have some idea of Him no doubt, but it's so vague: nature, our country, the world— all the things that take on a full and true meaning for us only because we find in them the presence of God, of the Father, of the Word and of Love. With the help of a religious sense whose force and joy they do not suspect, we can accept everything, understand everything, and praise everything. I keep recalling the last lines of the "Song of the Night Watchman":

Der Wind pocht an mein Fenster
und spricht vom lieben Gott.

The wind knocks at my window
and talks to me of God.

But I know that all our work—and this whole factory— is helping the war. I know that the screws we have just polished will complete the plane that will soon be off to spread death in England or elsewhere. I can feel this thought weighing heavily on us, so that at times we long to smash our machines.

But I believe that Christ's triumph hasn't been in vain and that God bends Satan himself to manifest His glory. I believe more than ever in Pascal's three orders, with charity dominating and infinitely surpassing the order of matter. I believe that the parts that leave my hands, sabotaged to the small degree my work permits, will bring more love than hatred to the world, and more peace than war. I believe my actions have other echoes in the world than the bursting of bombs, because it's up to me, through the Holy Ghost that *dwells within us, to make of them a prayer of adoration, peace, and love.*

January 6, 1944 (Epiphany)

Happy to be able to offer again today, for a shortening of the long wait of the peoples of the world for the great Epiphany of the last day—when our tight little world will open, and the splendor and love of Christ, which has been silently growing in the hearts of peoples, will finally burst forth. Then the peoples' leaders, who now seem to guide the world, will come forward and will meet Christ—perhaps to their joy, perhaps to their damnation. Reges de Saba venient, Reges Tharsis et insulae munera offerent ("Kings will come from Saba, kings of Tharsis and the islands will offer Him gifts").

Above all there will appear like a river of gold and fire the expectation of millions of men who have suffered in prisons and dungeons and camps, who accepted their sufferings and offered them up in their hearts. For me it's nothing; a month's prison is just an escapade. But what about our prisoners, what about the deportees, what about the people in concentration camps—what about them? If the weight of their expectation and wretchedness and the cry of their hope were converted into gold coins, or light, or harmony, the whole earth would be shaken to its foundations, it would throb with heart-rending and glorious music. On the day of the great Epiphany, we shall have eyes and ears for those things—we shall know them for reality as God now knows them, seeing and hearing them. . . .

I have no bread to offer, but a day in prison is a precious offering in my hands; I have no chalice to offer, but I have the hands of all the priests in the world offering it for me. I feel sure this must be why I suffer so little in not being able to celebrate Mass physically. I thought it was going to be a cruel privation, but in practice the Church is so alive in my cell, and I feel myself so carried along and supported by her, that the absence of the offices and ceremonies is not too painful.

Besides, how could I have any nostalgia for the services we knew only too well in France—those "private" and mechanical prayers which are mostly routine, those low Masses said by a solitary priest and attended by a few of the faithful, lost in the four corners of an almost empty church, or, almost worse, those worldly Masses with the spirit of prayer almost entirely gone out of them. I suffer more and more as I remember how the services and ceremonies have lost almost all meaning for the Christian people—one might almost say all sacredness, since so often Christians don't even receive Communion any more, and the sacramentals produce no effect (or very little). Our liturgy is weighted down with a thousand externals; it expresses the decorum of a bourgeois and pedestrian tradition, beneath which the living prayer of the Church is stifled; it has no hold on the Christian people, since it no longer expresses their life and prayer. The liturgy, which should be the living expression of the prayer of God's people, is almost dead in most of our churches. I recall Masses where people fell asleep, where everyone sat bored in total inertia, where the alms boxes, the seat offering, the collection, and the sermon spoke of nothing but money. . . .

Perhaps one day we'll be able to live another liturgy, springing spontaneously from the heart of a priestly people gathered round their high priest in a moving dialogue and communal act. On behalf of the world, the whole of suffering mankind, expressed in a little bread and wine, would be offered up in order to make of it the Body of Christ which purifies and sanctifies the world. The Mass must be made something alive, in which priest and people act, confess, receive instruction, sing and pray; in which priest and people achieve communion and are fused more and more in Christ. We must constantly keep in mind those others who neither can nor want to be there; Mass is a real mystery of unity, love, and redemption, food for rough men from farms and factories, for twenty-year-olds looking for adventure and risk. Our hymns of thanksgiving are to be to the scale of the whole world, like the famous prayers of the Didache or of Serapion: "Lord, let Thy Church be gathered together from the ends of the earth, in Thy kingdom," or like that psalm the Church has us say after Mass, and which I am always repeating here in prison: "All ye works of the Lord, bless the Lord." Let there be an end to those little devotional acts centered in self, to those ridiculous hymns which we mumbled as children in our first Communion retreat. . . .

It's sad to think that we have no Church hymns (except those of the Cité des Jeunes*—but what a revolution if we sang those in church!) in which we might "shout from the rooftops" the joys of our baptism, the joy of being strengthened and possessed by the love of Christ, or the rich joy of a married couple in discovering their love and offering it in homage to God. Instead, we have hymns to the Virgin in deplorable taste, hymns to the Blessed Sacrament of absurd sentimentality and watered-down dogma, often set to "chewing-gum" music. . . .

* A young Catholic group organized in Paris by Fr. Filler.

But one day the Epiphany will burst upon us, and all the
peoples will sing. . . .

End of January, 1944

Beyond the limitations and depressions the body suffers
from, I feel astonishingly and profoundly free; I feel the
flame and secret life of an inalienable freedom beating within
me. They can keep me under lock and key, they can lead
me off to a concentration camp tomorrow, they can torture
me till I howl with pain, but they can't touch the sanctuary
where my spirit is on the watch and where I am sole and
absolute master. They can deceive me, abuse me, weaken
me, and get out of my shaky mind words they'll take for an
abdication of myself; they can kill me, but they can't get at
my freedom, for it doesn't belong to them—it's something
between God and myself and no one else can touch it.

What makes them think it's so easy to reduce a Christian
to slavery, or to tie down Christian activity with chains, walls,
and warders? On the contrary, in the last month I've seen
with ever-increasing certainty that I can do more for our
young Christians within the four walls of my cell than on
the week ends I used to devote to some Catholic Action
group.

Only one thing could stifle the burning flame of the
Spirit that lives within me, and that is sin or despair; but in
that case I would have put out the fire with my own hands
and forged my own chains. As long as I am faithful to God
I am the freest man in the world and nothing and no one
can enslave me. . . .

My companions are amazed at the astonishing freedom I
feel. If they knew what a Christian is, they would, rather,
be amazed that I am still so affected by the slavery of my

body. *If they knew I was Christ's member, they'd be amazed,
rather, at seeing me still a slave to so many things, though
He came to free us from them.* . . .

But temptations and doubts, inevitable in the circumstances, naturally followed periods of such exaltation:

*My companions seem to make off as soon as the question
of religion is broached; they're like people forced to drink
something which has made them sick before, or asked to
wear something they'd stowed away in the attic because it
was tight and out-of-date.* . . .

*It is only by a constant effort—thanks to my long years of
Christian training and to the way in which circumstances
worked together to make me feel the need for God and a
sense of my own inadequacy—that I keep the thought of
God in the forefront of my mind. Among my companions
the absence of any interest in religion amounts almost to
pure and simple negation, and if one lived alone in this
atmosphere one might begin to wonder if they weren't
right.*

*"Supposing the question didn't really arise?"—this is
what one of our Rovers asked Jacques after six months' contact with the materialism of his Russian comrades. Suppose
the question of religion were only a false problem which
only concerned those who, through weakness or tradition or
the influence of their environment, are "in it"? There are
long hours when my mind is filled with doubts; how must it
be for others who are "emancipated" and live in surroundings in which everything ignores God—the press and business, love and philosophy, engineering and education—how
can they be open to any religious interest when not only*

their own life but all of life around them is "Godless"?

Raymond and the others admit that it's something that has never crossed their minds; they never think of God even as a problem. Once they've said that, I can't treat them as Christians; they not only do not "practice" Christianity, they haven't the faintest desire to practice it; they pretty well never adopt the Christian position on the great problems that inevitably present themselves to a man as soon as he thinks—life, love, money, death, society, the family, justice. So how can I call them Christians? I've told them so, frankly and firmly. They are not Christians and they have no right to claim the title, since they have nothing to do with Christ. It would be reducing the word to mean a mere origin, like saying a sardine is Spanish or Moroccan!

Whether they mean to or not, they live in utter paganism. Although they've been baptized and lived for a while in a Christian environment, bit by bit they've lost the tastes, needs, reflexes, and convictions of a Christian. Just as the Christianization of a pagan environment is achieved progressively, by stages that can hardly be detected, so the paganization of a Christian environment occurs imperceptibly, as autumn leaves change their color, slowly die, and fall from the tree.

Robert, Charles, Henri, Remi, Marcel, Michel, Roger, René, and Hermanus—like nearly everyone else I've met both here and at the factory—have to be treated like pagans in the sense that there's no question of "recalling them to their Christian duties." What has to be done is to awaken in them the desire to be Christians. Since I've been in prison I've heard only two confessions, and even then it was I who made the suggestion. There seems little point in talking to them about the sacraments, although these are the wonder of the Christian life; but I must talk to them about God, Christ, their souls, the Church, eternity—exactly as if I were dealing with Chinese mandarins, Russian workers, or American students. This is obviously harder than when these things are taken for granted and you benignly remind them of their duty or exhort them to virtue. You have to commit yourself and reveal the depths of your soul. In our so-called Christian environment we speak of Christ, of the things of God, of the inner life of the soul, in traditional and conventional terms, in recognized places and at certain hours, and with discretion, reserve, and a certain shyness. Whereas we should say, "I believe in Jesus Christ," as shamelessly as Raymond says, "I believe in money," or Ilia, "I believe in Stalin," or our SS adjutant, "I believe in my Fuehrer."

This morning I was given the job of drilling holes in the cement around the edge of the terrace. I worked gently away with my pick and mallet, my legs hanging over the edge, thirty yards from the ground, facing the crossroads a hundred yards away between the police headquarters and the courthouse. We often come to look at it, like children looking out of the window when their mother has forbidden them to go out—that is always the time when the road seems liveliest and most full of people and adventure.

With hands in our pockets and eyes fixed on the crossroads, we stand for a long time watching life rushing past us in the heart of the city. Germans in all sorts of uniforms, cartloads of Ukrainian women, groups of French, English, and Russian prisoners of war, International Red Cross cars with Swiss or Swedish soldiers in them, conscripts of every nation looking for information, people from every country of Europe meeting before us at this crossroads.

You get the feeling that the world has suddenly shrunk, and that people who yesterday were comfortably settled in their own little corners are now being hurled together in some sort of decisive encounter.

I recall a Christmas evening a few years ago on Lake Tiberias, when English, Germans, and French all sang songs of their countries around a lighted Christmas tree.

Crossroads, meetings: yesterday by chance on a journey, today in war, tomorrow in work. The world which used to seem so vast has now become a single workyard where mankind labors together. The time is coming when everyone must think on a world scale—leave his house, his village, his province, his country—and learn to be a brother to everyone in the world. I refuse to admit that the roads of the world must cross only in hatred, dividing peoples and classes. I am convinced that many tendencies explained as laws of history are often the result of ignorance, obstinacy, or more or less conscious prejudices—that is, when they do not arise from political factions or economic interests.

Our hearts are not Christian enough to make a social revolution in the name of the Gospel, and we have failed in our mission to bring unity in the social sphere. We must not fail in the future in the international sphere. . . .

We should be known by our passionate consciousness of, and desire for, world unity. That's our duty as Christians and should be our honor as Frenchmen. For both these reasons we should make it our business in the future to be in the vanguard of international world organization.

Are we ready for it? The very idea is a joke. As Frenchmen we are almost completely bound up in our own language and country, and we have to force ourselves to go abroad or to learn another language. As Christians we seem equally uninterested in the idea of unity, judging by our insensibility in recent years to divisions among Christians, to schisms and heresies, to the tragic rendings of Christ's Body. Things are beginning to improve, but the movement toward unity in the Church is still, for most priests and most Catholics, far from a real preoccupation.

Finally we must quote from the *Diary* his appeal to the German people:

> You, the German people, are holding me here;
> You killed my father before I even knew him;
> You carry the weight of ten years' accumulated crime;
> You have become the nightmare of Europe and of the world by three times starting wars;
> Your brutality, pride, and felony have shed the blood of countless families.
>
> I know that soon you will be dismembered and dispersed, that the work of justice has scarcely begun, and that you must pay hard for the crimes of some of your sons; your pain must last for a long time to expiate all you have done.
>
> Others will have the job of pronouncing justice over you; the only thing asked of me is to pray for you, according to Our Lord's command: "Love your enemies; do good to them that hate you; pray for them that persecute and calumniate you."
>
> I have loved your youth and your songs and the heroism you bring to the service of your faith, even though you worship false idols;
>
> I have loved your unsatisfied heart, your respect for order, and your cult of community;
>
> I have loved the welcome of your children, and especially

of your priests, and I have realized how often the hating
voices that wish to oppose us are lying;

And more than ever I want to pray:

Father,
who hast created this people, who hast made them Thy
sons, and the sons of Thy Church;

I know Thou lovest them as much as Thou lovest us;

I know that they, too, are called to sing Thy glory, to
found Thy kingdom, and to sanctify the world;

I know that their nation has had many saints, in whom
the Church eternally rejoices, beginning with their Em-
peror Henry, who was given me as my patron;

I know that for ten years they, too, have offered Thee
martyrs.

Father, in union with the prayer of my first Mass, when
for the first time I offered up the chalice which bore
Christ's monogram, the insignia of the German Catholic
Youth,

In union with the prayers going up now from the
prisons and camps of this very people,

We will say the prayer given us in the Missal for our
enemies: "O God of peace, lover and guardian of charity,
give to all our enemies true charity and peace, grant them
the remission of all their sins, and mightily deliver us from
their machinations. Through Our Lord Jesus Christ Thy
Son, who liveth and reigneth with Thee, world without
end. Amen."

To complete my prayer, let me offer these months in
prison, my only riches, through the hands of Henry, Boni-
face, and the Archangel Michael, the patrons of Germany,
through the hands of Our Lady and of Christ;

And if I am to die without seeing my country again, if the offering of my life is to be added to those of so many others for the salvation of the world, grant that I may offer it to my Master with joy, when my sister death comes to fetch me, happy to offer my last sacrifice for them, that they may know Thee and love Thee, they and my brothers in France.

Perhaps there are friends who won't understand my prayer, who may feel that it's inopportune and embarrassing. I know how hard it is for us to think two things at the same time; but I also know that this prayer is rising from a German prison, and that it is during our moments of great temptation, when we risk spiritual blindness, that we have to cling to truth; and when we feel our hatred rising, that we have to pray for charity. And I know that far from condemning us, many of the unbelievers are waiting for us to teach them how to pray and forgive, asking us, as Christians, not to howl with the wolves, but to walk on the highroads ahead of them, carrying the light to free them from the dark.

And his vision of Christianity at work:

In a world suffering as it has never suffered, exhausted as it has never been exhausted, the Church prepares herself in the depths of Christ's life. Christians are growing up who understand the riches of their faith—baptism, marriage, and holy orders, and the Bread they partake of each day at Mass. They will bring their discovery of love and marriage to the world. They will not fear death, but will await it as a promise; they will choose for themselves a hard and joyful way of life, in poverty to the point of sharing everything they have. In a word, they will be Christians of a kind to draw all men of good will after them.

All this calls for men who can get out of themselves, who will cease walking solitary paths and come to the highroads where men of all nations pass by. Such Christians as these, leaping over the present rottenness of the world at a bound, will stand up before men, bearing the light of Christ past the winding ways and false mysticisms which mislead them.

This also calls for us to leave the ghetto in which we so often shut ourselves up—in our churches, our papers, our movements, our good works. . . .

III

Drawing the Lesson
(1944 – 1946)

When Henri Perrin was expelled from Germany in the early summer of 1944, he went to live at Action Populaire, the Jesuit house at Vanves, a Paris suburb.* But his heart was still with the deportees in Germany, as the following three letters to a friend show:

Vanves, June 1, 1944

My dear friend. You ask me for some of my impressions. Here they are, the outcome of prolonged thought.

Our Lord placed us for a few months in the heart of a foreign land, in order that we could testify to Him there, in order that we could be Him—that is to say, continue his work, in order that through us, by us, and in us He could speak and show Himself to the world.

* This is a lively Jesuit center of social studies, which also publishes a periodical entitled *Revue de l'action populaire.*

But make no mistake—this foreign land I'm talking about isn't the land to which we were suddenly transported, the country in which we lived. No, it's the workers' world, about which we previously knew nothing and which we gradually discovered while we were there.

For a long time, as good sons of France, we thought of all places except our own country as terra aliena. Like so many others, when we arrived in Germany we looked toward the West and thought of France, our France, our fatherland. It was natural enough.

But little by little we managed to see beyond the purely physical horizon and to discern the real meaning of the terra aliena all around us. This is the land where Christ is unknown, where the name of God evokes no response; it's the land of men without God, whether they're Latin, Slav, or German. When we were young we docilely accepted what we were taught, always identifying France and the Church, singing at the tops of our voices, and with full conviction: "Catholic and French forever." But when we were in Germany various admissions were wrung out of us. In our new life we were obliged to see and reckon with the mass of ordinary people, non-Christians, those who are not "one of us," whom we had never come across before except in the silence of the streets, on buses, or in trams. Suddenly, as a result of a conversation or a meeting, or a meditation while digging, we discovered a "foreign country"—which yesterday was distant and unknown, but today terribly close and terribly distressing.

Terra aliena, those volunteer workers who were there before me and for whom my presence didn't raise the slightest challenge.

Terra aliena, those men, transformed by circumstances,

who haven't time for a word with you because every evening
they are driven by the demands of sex.

Terra aliena, those fellow workers whose hate talk I cannot accept and who, for that reason, feel I am on the "other
side."

Terra aliena, those fellow workers who have slowly fallen
into habits of dishonesty and theft; or foreigners separated
from me by the language barrier and whose distress I therefore cannot estimate.

Terra aliena, those whose contempt penetrated me like
an icy fog—because I belong to Christ and his Church.

As the only Christian among pagans, as a witness to the
Master to whom I drew closer every day, I got to know the
terra aliena very well indeed. My astonished eyes scrutinized
it from every point of view; but far from feeling the distress
of an exile, my heart leapt with joy and gratitude. Lord, you
have set us down in an unknown land so that we can be
Yourself there.

And it's true that this pagan multitude has been entrusted
to us as our domain. Far from dominating us, these godless
men are in our hands, for the most part poor creatures who
ask for light and friendship. Yes, of course, they won't be
coming to Mass next Sunday, and it's much better that they
shouldn't. But they need a Christian near them, someone
who is attractive and doesn't think like everyone else, who
behaves in a way that is a witness to the existence of another
world where life is happier because people believe in something beyond themselves. I've seen them full of astonish-
ment and admiration when they learned about our prayers,
our friendship, and our faith. We may not be much in ourselves, but at least they've met Christians, a thing that
doesn't happen every day....

Vanves, July 1, 1944

*My Dear. What are you up to? The weary routine, or
revolt? Perhaps both.* I must admit that throughout the
eight months that Christ involved me, like you, in the terra
aliena I was talking about the other day, my dominant impression was an immense need for greatness and strength.
Whether I was faced with the workmate who said, "No, I
don't think religion's what's wanted for rebuilding the
country—the clergy's too corrupt"; or with the challenging
faith of the Party members; or with the attractive but delu-
sive freedom of those who thought of themselves as emancipated; or with the civil servant who said to me, "It's a pity
you devote your energies to such a poor cause as Catholicism"; or with "Bordeaux," a toughie nicknamed after the
town he comes from, who said contemptuously, "I have a
strong feeling we're not of the same kind" (his hatred
seemed so strong compared with the pale Catholic "charity"
incurably rigged out in stuffy, out-of-date and impotent
forms); or with powerful specimens of humanity such as
Russians or Germans; or with the light-hearted carelessness
of the "upper-class young men" educated in our colleges;
everywhere, endlessly, I was beset by the same painful impression: In the eyes of the world our Christianity has lost
nearly all its value; it has become something aged and vener-
able, but powerless—a little shop for people already provided for, and run by priests whom no one blames for making a living as best they can.

For some, our Christianity is a nonproducer, for others a
tired and worn-out body, for many a small matter that is
quite apart from life and the vital impulses that sweep
people and things forward. Confronted with the real world,
in the eyes of those around us, the Catholic seems branded

with an inferiority complex, and Nietzsche's sarcasms, repeated by the world at large, seem to fall on him.

We who see things from within and have marveled at
the splendor of dogma, and experienced the Father's caress
and the Church's tenderness—we know what sort of building we are looking at and we believe in the kingdom. But the
others have only seen Christianity from the sidelines, as a
business of money collections and funerals, a business for
sacristans and old maids. We can't blame them, for it's
surely up to us to present them with a different picture. . . .

I've been amazed to realize how—even in the most every-
day circumstances—total Christianity demands challenging
words and actions, a practical attitude toward squalor, suffering, and death, an affirmation of our faith in life, love,
and the next world. Think how many of Christ's precepts
are a dead letter for us these days. "Do good to those that
harm you. . . . I was naked and you clothed me not. . . . Turn
the other cheek"; or think of the precepts of John the Baptist at the beginning of the Gospel of St Luke: "Let the man
who has two garments give one to the man who has none."
Some people have everything, others have literally nothing
—and Christians are often complacently installed between
the two. . . .

Vanves, July 15, 1944

My Dear. I spent hours last night with a group of labor
conscripts like you. You can imagine how happy I was to
make contact again. The main thing we talked about was
their reunions; they agreed unanimously that these were ab-
surdly artificial, and that with all the will in the world they
were bored to death. We tried to trace the causes and found
that what is lacking is any genuine community spirit among

them—to carry them on, draw them together, unite them, nourish them, and make them into a team whose meetings would take place as often as possible and be a need as well as a source of strength and joy.

As I listened to them, my thoughts strayed to letters that have come here, and I thought of the experiments made in the past year by so many groups, and in the past five years in various stalags: in almost all instances men have been found who reformed the community from within—a community slowly founded on friendship and joy, slowly welded together in endeavor and love.

At school we experienced friendship through common effort and discovery: a fine sports team, a study group, perhaps a group of apostles. But now the field of experience has opened up beyond measure and we experience community in innumerable areas: genuine community that may begin with a "goodly noise" and a decently cooked meal, decently shared (basis of the mysticism surrounding sacrificial meals in all religions; but how different Mass is today from the Last Supper!); community in manual work undertaken and completed by four or five men together—we've all experienced and enjoyed that, and it's often seemed to me as heady as wine. But above all, you, like me, have perhaps been staggered by the discovery of the workers' community, or rather, the community of the proletariat—the tremendous, almost unconscious force that fills the air in the main hall of a factory or that breathes among men in morning trams and trains. Have you experienced this community strength on entering or leaving a factory, when you are in the crowd—the impression of unity and terrible force that grips men and rolls them on irresistibly, like a mountain torrent? I remember how it hurt me when I asked a Czech whether he was a Christian and he said: "What does religion matter? We're all workers." When you've felt the force of the workers' community, what a pitiable impression of weakness you get when you speak of the Christian community; the thought of the spiritless and tired life of practicing Catholics hovering around their parish priest merely raises a smile.

We realize all this, but we also realize that the Christian community, as it exists at present and is seen by the pagans who surround us, is only a caricature—sometimes only fit to make you weep—of the Church we really cherish. That's why there is a need to create, at least among a few Christians, a real Christian community, intensely lived in all its demands—with its faith, passion, and power to astonish—so that pagans around us will be forced to say: "Look how they love one another."

And this isn't just hot air. We have lived it, felt it, seen it, with all the joy you can get at twenty from such an experience. Whether in some odd corner of a factory or farm or town or village, whenever a handful of Christians starts reforming the true Christian community, the whole pagan mass around them starts loving them and moving gently toward them, as a wounded man holds out his hand to you when you've lovingly washed, cleaned, and dressed an open wound.

I could give you dozens of examples. Some of us, including friends of yours, plan to tell you in a letter how we've experienced true community as expressed in an intense need for communal prayer, simple, direct, and brotherly. One of my own greatest joys during my eight months away was the marvelous community of feeling I had with Jacques, the Rover leader who went with me, also as a volunteer: com-

munity of work, of earnings, of meals, of an ideal long sought
for and pondered over together; community all along the
line, so that we became one in Christ.

I pray with all my heart that you'll find such total community with a comrade, and the joy of this vinculum cari-
tatis.

August and September of 1944 were months of feverish
activity throughout the whole of France: the Allied land-
ings, the German collapse, the liberation of Paris. Henri
lived through them quietly in his suburb—in striking con-
trast to his previous year. His own work absorbed him so
deeply that he seemed hardly touched by what was happening. He talks about his work in a letter to his Carmelite
cousin:

> 15 rue de Paris, Vanves, L'Action Populaire
>   October 5, 1944
> My very dear Sister. A free evening and my Office said.
> I'd meant to go on reading . . . but it's such a long time since
> I've written to you. . . .
> Throughout the Liberation I was engaged in writing up
> my Diary of a Priest-Worker in Germany and making it into
> a book, which will probably come out in a few months. I
> shall send you a copy. You will find there all my heart, all
> my enthusiasm, all my faith in the Church, and, I hope, all
> my tender love of Christ. You grumble at not having my
> news, so this time you'll have more than enough. You'll find
> all my preoccupations about the future, and my constant
> concern about the way we're separated from the people, the
> way we've become respectable, and how we lack the free-
> dom, the lightness, the love, and the charm of the Gospel.

You can't imagine how much I suffer almost every day at our ceremonies, our preaching, our bourgeois customs, our way of living apart—and this while the pagan masses are suffering and imploring someone to talk to them. I am more than ever convinced that the French masses have been paganized and that the witness of Christians is utterly inadequate.

Some sort of explosive reform is needed (which the Popes have been asking of us for years), but we don't bring it about for fear of going against "tradition" and routine. I am preparing myself slowly and deeply, and you can imagine that these thoughts only make me want further years of deeper preparation. But I sometimes wonder whether we'll get there in time to avoid having to work in the worst conditions. We're not yet ripe for a Communist revolution, but we'll be hard put to it to catch up on the others' start. It's terrible to feel we've been overtaken, and to see the rush toward catastrophe without being able to stop it.

A local parish priest near here, one among the few in Paris who have a real grasp of the work to be done, said the other day: "When you start trying to do a little, you see there's a whole world of change needed." I wish I could tell you how normal it is for the pagan world to see our life as that of good civil servants, calmly running their departments, and—taken all in all—not living too badly. . . .

I finished my book ten days ago, and now my main activity is learning English and German, with the idea of returning to Germany again. Abbé Rodhain has proposed that the Government should set up teams ready to go to Germany as soon as circumstances permit, to greet our comrades and organize their return home. I'll continue my letter on the back of one of the leaflets explaining this project, so that you'll see what it's about. So I'm all ready to go, but as I have to go to Leipzig I expect I shall only be off at the armistice, which may well be any time—perhaps next year! I shall wait until November and then if I see no sign of anything happening I shall be going to Lyons to begin my theology.

I feel confirmed in the aims I told you about. At the earliest possible moment I'll center my theological studies on God's life in our world through Christ. The Mystical Body, the Church, the priesthood of the faithful, confirmation, Catholic Action—I want to dig deeply into all these subjects. I'll be writing about this again.

At about this time the Abbé Godin's book, *France, Pays de Mission,* had wide repercussions among the younger and more enthusiastic French clergy. In his book the Abbé Godin analyzed, from firsthand knowledge, the outlook of the French working classes, and put forward ideas very similar to those maturing in Henri Perrin's mind. Godin's book was fundamental in the priest-worker movement.

Have been reading France, Pays de Mission. But why limit the problem to the proletariat, as though it alone were pagan? Are the working classes further from understanding the Mass and Christian externals than the middle classes or the peasants? Are there, from the point of view of religion, such deep differences between these classes as between the Negroes of the African missions and the French in our parishes? I don't know the real proletariat very well, but I can't see that between the environment of the workers and that of the middle classes and of the peasants there are differences to justify a special apostolate and clergy. The problem seems to be common to all our pagans from whatever environment they come. All feed on the same films, the same newspapers, the same magazines; their aspirations and tastes have much in common.

Early in the following year, 1945, Henri Perrin went to Germany to take part in the liberation of his deported comrades. Some time after his return to France he wrote about it to his Carmelite cousin:

Lyons, November 20, 1945

Very dear Sister. Pax Christi. You'd be cross with me if you knew that seven weeks ago I passed by your sleeping Carmelite convent by car at eleven at night.

As Mother will have told you, I've just finished a new plunge into active life, or rather into a roughhouse. For seven months I've been touring through north Germany as military chaplain in Abbé Rodhain's so-called Vatican mission. Besides a whole lot of other business, my main activity was contacting the German clergy and, from August onward, founding at Bonn an international Catholic center dealing with all Catholic interests in the British zone—with the Poles, who are still in exile, with German prisoners, evacuees, clergy, and university people. All I managed to do was to get the thing going, greatly helped by the British; then I handed it over to my successor, in order to take up my studies again.

Of course it was absorbing work, and in various ways a trial of strength—of spiritual life, sureness of judgment, sense of organization, and so on. In practice I lived an officer's life, with epaulettes, hotels, cars, etc. Making use of things as if you weren't making use of them. . . . How often

I kept asking myself what Christ would have done in my position. The frightening thing was the realization that, willing or not, in practice I had to be the living Christ there. One thing was, and still is, hard—the second vow, chastity. Despite everything, there are times when it is very hard. But after all it's normal and right that this should be so. To cut things short, I didn't go off the rails, but you can't imagine how much I appreciated feeling near to you and my Trappist brother. You are my two pillars.

Taking all things into consideration, I am convinced I've still got a long way to go before I become totally dedicated, without thought for myself. As for my activity over souls, there's a big gap to be filled in spite of appearances of success. The saints weren't like that.

So I'm glad to be taking up two more years of study and disciplined effort. I'm delighted to return to my books (I've just been rereading Matthew almost nonstop, and it's a revelation).

One little event has been the appearance of my first brainchild, which is causing a minor sensation and I feel doing a bit of good....

February 8, 1946

Some quick news. I'm carrying on with my theological studies and feel even more enthusiasm than before, partly because of a whole mass of things I thought were certain and now I find I have to question them again, and partly because of the problems and needs arising from my two stays in the heart of the non-Christian community. I've got a real hunger for study.

Since I got back from Paris the other day, I've felt more than ever that our religion, as it now exists, has ceased to correspond to what mankind is awaiting. Nonbelievers of perfectly good faith feel not the slightest attraction (very much the contrary) to Church things—priests, ceremonies, dogmas, etc., while believers are beginning to be disgusted with all they are made to do. Where is the "good news"?

It's really tragic; since it corresponds with a period in which I have had to overhaul all my beliefs, I've been asking myself for the first time in my life whether I wouldn't be obliged to raise the question of trust, and get involved in a crisis of belief. Things are a bit better now, but not without a struggle.

The solidest thing I have is the formidable presence of God, who at every moment, in the most intimate part of my being, is creating me in love, as well as the presence of Christ at the heart of the world—from which He formed his body and which He is slowly transforming by means of his Church. But what a mystery there is about all this! At the moment I'm studying original sin and the catechesis of St. Cyril of Jerusalem. I've just got going with the Epistle to the Romans. I feel as I did two years ago, when I began with the Epistle to the Ephesians, that I'm penetrating a field absolutely new and unknown to me. It will take me three months to begin to get the hang of it!

I'm getting quite a lot of letters about my Diary. I'm sure you'd like to see a few extracts!

From an Anarchist

I almost wanted to begin "Dear Friend" because of the great sympathy I feel with you. It would be difficult to explain why. Perhaps it's because of your desire for an absolute in love and truth. I'm like you in that; I have a horror of lies and approximations. Your religious order was one of the things I hated most, and now, because of you, my hatred has grown less. Of course, this won't make me a Catholic, but you have made me believe that there are real Christians in the Church such as Christ intended. I'd like to meet a lot of men like you (though I don't care about religion), because I'd like to live in a world in which love is the rule. I also feel the need to believe that man will become better, not by the force of things (that seems too mechanical to me) but because he has in him what is necessary for that. It's now two thousand years since Christ came to help men to live, and they're still the same as, if not worse than, before. So what are we to believe?

I envy you having faith; today is a feast day for you and your heart is full of joy. Thank you for coming to the house; you've given me a chance of being rather less unhappy because I'm writing to you as a friend, and that will make my Christmas. Thanks for that. Once I feel friendship, it's forever; you're my friend, if you want to be, for my whole life. I won't write often, I find writing too hard, but I'll often think of you and you'll know you have someone who will always be happy to see you again and help you as far as he can.

From a Luxemburgian woman doctor in Germany

I had plenty of opportunity during three years to study Germany and the Germans, since I was pretty closely involved with the Catholic student groups at Marburg. It was in Germany that my faith developed and grew intellectual roots. In fact it was in our students' circle at Marburg that I first heard of the liturgy and began to get interested in theology. Of course we had religious instruction at the lycée, but it was enough to make us fed up with the whole thing forever. Then there was the social question. I come from the industrial world; my grandparents were workers. I knew how far all that was from the Church. In your book you put your finger on all the questions we discussed so often at Marburg, which can be summed up in: "Has the Church failed or not?" Not, of course, as instituted by Christ; that can't perish, we have his word for it. But what men have made of it! "God's great adventure," Péguy called it. The meaning of Protestantism. The Eastern Church. Do you know Friedrich Heiler? He was at Marburg. That's why we talked so much about the Eastern Church. I got slightly involved in it, especially with the Russians.

And now a question. Do some of you seriously envisage going to Russia, as you went to Germany? And if so I daresay a little Catholic doctor who is now learning Russian would be useful to you. Of course I'm referring to myself, and seriously. . . .

From a captain in Germany

You touch on a crucial point when you indicate the responsibility of the clergy for the present state of religious sclerosis in France. If in both their interior and exterior life Catholics have failed to give an example, and failed to be apostles in their own sphere of influence, what can we say about the Church's sin of omission! For it's up to the Church to foresee and to organize—two prerogatives of a leader. If we don't want Christianity in France to die of inanition, methods will have to be radically changed, and from now on the elite of the clergy must show a capacity for decision. It surely isn't difficult to obtain right away a reform of the ceremonies, imprisoned as they are in framework of another age: a renewal of the arsenal of prayers and hymns, Mass in French and loud enough to be understood, a catechism that isn't a conundrum, preaching confined to priests capable of adapting their words to the needs of their listeners and of turning sermons into something other than sleeping pills or, by their insignificance, into counterpropaganda.

Another thing we need is that young priests should be sent out of the Catholic ghetto in ordinary clothes to join in the life of the country, presenting people with a virile and joyous Christianity. . . .

From a senior parish priest

Personally I'm fully aware that our methods in the apostolate are now out-of-date, and I'm full of admiration for the young priests who make every dynamic effort to win over the masses by involving themselves with them to the point of living their lives. Yet we are the slaves of the formation we received, and we feel incapable of following them along this road. We are tormented by our powerlessness. We pray God to bless this apostolate of the young, so excellently adapted to the present situation. . . .

From a Communist militant

We were laid very low, but what we lived through together was nothing to what I went through afterwards, and it was a real miracle—no, it was my physical strength and my hatred of the Nazis—that enabled me to hold out. I came back on crutches, for I deliberately chose to have my feet crushed in order to escape death. Since then I've been restored to health and activity. And I promise you that as soon as I've got a bit straight, I'll give myself the pleasure of inviting you to stay a few days. I'll stop now. Please give my regards to your Mother. I enclose a little money that you can give to some needy person. The dream of my life is far from being realized. We went through misery, and it's our duty to relieve the misery of others.

To his Carmelite cousin

Mongré, March 28, 1946

My very dear Sister. At last I'm getting down to writing you. I was waiting for the extracts from letters to come from Paris. Here they are at last. . . . These months are being extraordinarily profitable to me, and when I think that I have twelve more in front of me I feel overwhelmed—better than the best of consolations. Don't worry, the life of study is not uncongenial to me at all; I wanted it and expect a lot from it; yet I'll surely be far from getting from it all that it could give me.

Another grace that Our Lord has had in store for me is making me touch the very limits of my capacities, and this in several directions; it isn't always fun, but it's healthy. I'm quite terrified to realize how much holiness and intelligence is needed in the mission that awaits us. We must go forward, eyes shut, in mutual trust and in interdependence. Which is to say that, more than ever, I count on you.

Our plan for Holy Week is coming along admirably. I almost had to give it up because of the train fares. But finally we decided we'd get to Frébécourt somehow, even if it meant hitchhiking. There'll be about twenty of us altogether, a dozen men students and six or seven girl students. They are extremely keen, and are busy preparing the week without my having to do anything. I'll send you the program as soon as it's printed so that you can follow us step by step with your prayers. I hope to visit you during the evening

of Easter Monday, and perhaps in the first days of Holy
Week. Mother will be with me on Monday. I'm expecting
her to arrive in Frébécourt on the Wednesday of Holy
Week. . . .

Unnecessary for me to say that all your intentions are
mine, as mine are yours. I entrust especially to your prayers
the son of the American woman [Maisie Ward] who is in
charge of the English edition of my Diary; her little Wil-
frid, aged fifteen, is bedridden with infantile paralysis.

Rest with God, my Sister. Through your prayer, mine
spreads out to the ends of the earth. It seems strange to say
that, when I think of what I am, and yet. . . . May we be
united, as He is with his Father.

IV

Toward a Personal Vocation

(1946 – 1947)

AFTER the Holy Week experiment in Frébécourt in the Vosges and before attending a Congress on the Apostolate to the Working People, Henri Perrin wrote to one of his Superiors, explaining his ideas on the apostolate in a pagan environment, and affirming his personal vocation.

To Father W.

June 22, 1946

What I am expecting from the Congress is an opportunity for people to meet each other and for the problem to be raised. As for a solution, that will have to wait for ten years.

As I see it, the problem is not so much that of the paganized environment as that of our environment and its institutions, how it conforms to the requirements of a truly apostolic life. By our environment I mean religious and ecclesiastical circles, or even simply Christian ones, which, more and more, the nonbelievers of our day just will not swallow.

They are often attracted by the doctrine, and by the spiritual vitality, but the whole setup and its institutions repel them.

Where "penetration and witness" are mentioned, I would rather say "purification and return to the Gospels." I don't mean to imply by this that we have abandoned the Gospels, but that the general state of unbelief as it is now—even in a country still completely furnished with Christian institutions—demands that we rediscover the Gospels, with the maximum possible concentration, simplicity, and spirituality.

As Abbé Michonneau himself says in Revolution in a City Parish, his missionary parish is still only a halfway house, necessary because parishes exist in France. I do not see how these parishes, as they now stand, can ever gather in the unbelieving masses; but on the day when they lived by the authentic spirit of the Gospel, they would immediately be very different, and then they would quite naturally draw in the waiting masses.

But all that will take a long time, and I think we must tackle the problem in another way. Nothing makes us more aware of our deficiencies and of the demands of the Gospel than living in the heart of the pagan environment and having to instill the good news into it. And that is first and foremost what I desire.

From Father W. to Henri Perrin

L'Action Populaire, Vanves
October 1, 1946

Very dear Father. A number of the participants in the Congress on the Apostolate to Paganized Environments have said that they would like to keep in touch with each other, and have asked Action Populaire to serve as a center. I have readily agreed.

To make and keep this contract, I would like each of you in the course of the year to let me know your reflections, desires, and experiences, so that I can communicate them to all the others. And I will add my own documentation when necessary. For instance I am today forwarding you a copy of the preface that Cardinal Suhard has just written for the second edition of Revolution in a City Parish. It can hardly fail to interest you. But I would just like to draw your attention to one or two points.

People are already making use of the Cardinal's few reservations to prove that his preface shows disapproval of Michonneau's work and ideas. As the Cardinal has spoken to me at length on the subject, I can tell you exactly what he thinks. He has made such reservations as he has, precisely to enable the book to make an impact, despite the attacks to which it has been subjected in certain quarters. He told me that he is convinced of the necessity of tackling pagan environments boldly and with new methods that still need to be perfected, and he added that he is counting a great deal on the Society of Jesus to help him think out these problems. In a word, he has decided to go ahead despite opposition, and would feel he was failing in his duty as a bishop if he did not do so. His main idea at the present moment more or less tallies with the one we reached at the end of the Congress. He envisages the organization of a territorial apostolate, with the parish priest of the territory having responsibility for all souls (Christian and pagan alike) and, with this end in view, having at his disposal two sorts of clergy: a parish clergy whose function is to give life to a missionary

parish with a vigorous Catholic Action organization, and a
missionary clergy entrusted with penetrating the pagan environment with methods that have to be adapted in each
particular case and in association with the Catholic Action
of the parish. The Cardinal developed similar ideas in the
talk he gave a few days ago to his clergy at their pastoral retreat. I'll forward you the text of this talk as soon as I get
it. . . .

At about the same period Henri noted down his very
strong reactions to a parish mission:

1. The suggestions put forward are excellent as far as they
go, but in my humble opinion they're about as practical as
bandaging up a wooden leg. To treat the problem by means
of the traditional type of mission seems to me out of the
question.

2. The solution of the problem seems to me to demand a
totally new method, rethought with the environment in
mind. (It's more than a question of vocabulary and lantern
slides!) Three weeks' work along these lines would open
people's minds—even Christians'—to the problem of
prayer, the sacramental system, and the Mass, to go no
further.

We must:

a. Make ourselves keenly aware of the life problems of
a given environment (social conditions, justice, family,
future, etc.).

b. Draw up a working plan on the basis of these reali-
ties.

c. Introduce elementary religious experiences: prayer,
belief in God, community.

d. Once souls have been aroused, outline and bring to light the main lines of the Christian mystery centered around baptism (the notion of divinization), and Mass (seen as the sacrifice of the world, bound up with this divinization), and of marriage (a crucial point).

3. But above all, and first and foremost, it seems to me useless and even harmful to give a mission to the masses without lengthy preparation with the parish priest and the Christians of the area.

Otherwise, the best plan would be to hold a real mission for the sixty-odd Christian militants and their families— quietly carried out. It would be much more effective.

But to hold a mission of the traditional type in an environment like that—no.

Henri always put his holidays to good account, and thanks to his letters to his Carmelite cousin we can follow his itinerary:

Maria-Laach, August 12, 1946

My very dear Sister. Thank you for your long letter. I'm glad I provided the opportunity for you to know of the movement for the reunion of the Churches. Pray first and foremost that the clergy, and especially the clergy of Rome, may enter into the movement and appreciate the acuteness of the problem.

Here I am at the abbey of Maria-Laach, where I've been a Benedictine for three weeks, practicing German—reading and conversation. It's very difficult to get really inside a language. Tomorrow I'm leaving the abbey for Bonn and a tour of the American zone. I shall be coming back at the end of September to Tübingen to see Guardini, and then again

next year. On the 25th I'm due back in Paris for a few days
at the Action Populaire. At the beginning of September I go
to Lourdes for the pilgrimage of repatriated people, then
back to Paris again until the end of September. Later, Paris
again for an exam in German, then Belgium—Enghien—
for my last year of theology. Your prayers accompany me. I
count on you more and more and am in deep communion
and affection with you in Christ.

At this period Henri Perrin began taking an active part
in the international movement aimed at introducing
evening Mass. He had already written about it in his *Diary*
as follows:

If we want the Mass to become once more the prayer of
the Christian people, and if we want Christians to be able
to give the world the food it needs, we will have to get back
to the Last Supper, to evening Mass. Only custom and routine can keep us from feeling the urgency of this need.

It is absurd that Mass and Communion should have become the monopoly of people who have nothing to do, of
old women and the bourgeois. Rovers or militants in the
ranks of the J.O.C. or the J.A.C., who are at the heart of the
fight, will try in vain to give the world the Christian witness
it needs unless they are fed as often as possible on the Body
of Christ. Still more so, as Mass and Communion are not
only for them but for the whole environment—the district,
the factory, the block of flats, or group—over which Christ
has put them in charge. As things stand at present, with
Mass in the morning, they find attendance impossible. But
there's no reason why Christians should die of hunger today
because people didn't see the necessity yesterday. And I'm

sure that eight out of ten of the Christian militants who are at present working in German camps, as well as many others in France, are demanding this food.

Furthermore, communal life is coming more and more to be concentrated in the evenings. It's from 7 to 11 at night that the world comes alive, breathes, or at least tries to live. The morning hours are devoted to individual life—washing, dressing, getting ready for the day. I'm sure this is partly why the Mass has become such a solitary individualistic affair. It has lost nearly all its liturgical meaning. And anyway it's absurd that a woman working in a factory should have to get up at 5:30, rush to Mass at 6 to get Christ's strength, and then struggle to work at 7.

Whereas the evening is supremely the time of being together, of reunion, family life, meals in common. With a little good will it would be so easy to revive the atmosphere of the Last Supper. Our militants, who sometimes spend three or four evenings a week at meetings or engagements of some kind, could really make use of an evening with Christ, with the Church, in the offering and communion of the Christian sacrifice. It is often lamented that at solemn Mass on Sunday our people can't really enter into the magnificent, secret, and profound life of the Mass, of prayer, and of the priest's gestures. Let them be given the chance to come in the evening—even just three of them, or eight, or ten—to pray around their priests, around their altar, around their table, and in twenty years it would be a very different picture.

Rovers and J.O.C. members should demand it from their priests and bishops. It's their right, and the Church will be the first to rejoice when asked in this way. It's our inertia and routine that stand in the way.

Members of the Church already working for evening Mass included Mgr. Rastouil of Limoges, who had obtained special concessions from the Pope, abbés Cardijn and Guérin of the J.O.C. movement in Belgium and France, and the German bishops. Henri Perrin, with several friends, drew up a special petition and appealed for the signatures of four hundred militants and movement leaders:

Most Holy Father. Permit us to address ourselves in a filial way to you, in the name of Catholic groups and movements in France of which we are members, to tell you with what confidence we desire and await permission, as asked for by our cardinals and bishops, for evening Mass and Communion.

As you know, Most Holy Father, present conditions of life render morning Mass impossible for most of us, and in many parishes the priest has to celebrate almost alone the sacrifice which is the offering of the whole Christian community.

You know also the extent to which, in all environments, the Catholic Action militants feel they are responsible for the non-Christians among whom they live. You know with what tenacity and determination, sometimes at the cost of grave sacrifice to family and professional commitments, we meet together in our free time in the evenings, and late into the night, for reflection and prayer. You know how some of us, in recent years, have rediscovered the unforgettable atmosphere and strength of the Last Supper.

Most beloved Father, grant that our hours of meeting and of intense Christian community may sometimes also be hours of communion in which we can partake with our shepherd of the bread which we need, which we feel more and more necessary for our families, our movements, and the whole world around us—the bread that our Saviour told us is the Life of the World.

We are not asking for a new discipline regarding the Mass; all we wish is that, side by side with what already exists, there should be—under the authority of our pastors and, for instance, at a simple request to the bishop—the possibilty of offering the Sacrifice in the evenings.

We ask for this, most Holy Father, under the authority of our bishops, to whom we have submitted the more detailed report which we append. We ask you in the name of thousands of militants in our movements who would like to sign this petition with us; we ask it of you in the name of the Church, in which and through which we live in your paternal affection and benediction. From the Christians of France.

The communication to the Assembly of Cardinals and Archbishops of France on the subject of the petition differs very little from the petition to the Pope. Further developments are described in the following letter to an editor of the avant-garde Catholic weekly, *Témoignage Chrétien:*

... A word on the subject of our petition for evening Mass. It was taken to Rome on the 10th by Abbé Rodhain, who delivered it. It had three or four hundred signatures of heads or militants in the various Catholic movements. A few days later I received a letter from Mgr. Chapoulie which told me of the reaction of the Assembly of Cardinals and Archbishops. They were sympathetic, but felt "it was not opportune to send this petition because the Assembly itself had already raised similar questions with the Roman Congregations; and the French Cardinals, at the time of their visit to Rome, spoke personally to the Holy Father about it and even delivered a letter on the problem signed by themselves. At its last meeting, and in view of the feeling expressed in the petition, the Assembly decided to address a letter to the Holy Father raising the question with him again. This letter was signed by all the Cardinals and Archbishops present."

This letter (from Mgr. Chapoulie) arrived too late. Cardinal Suhard, whose advice I had asked on November 8, had merely said that the Assembly didn't want to sponsor the petition because it overlapped with what it was itself asking for, but that he saw no difficulty in our sending it privately. Taken all in all, things have gone well, for there has been both the petition and a letter from the Cardinals—and this last I could never have hoped for!

I really can't do an article on the subject for Témoignage Chrétien, at least not before the beginning of January. I'd rather send you the two relevant documents to make use of as you think fit. I think it would be better if you wrote the article. . . .

At this time (autumn 1946) Henri Perrin went to Enghien, Belgium, to resume his theology. And it was now that, in order to keep in touch with all his friends in Germany, Paris, and Lyons, he started writing collective letters—not often, but they are very valuable for showing the development of his thought and action. They cover slightly different ground from his letters to his Carmelite cousin:

Enghien, November 20, 1946
My Friends. I'm writing to all of you through Jacques. The letter can be circulated and perhaps be typed by Made-

leine. In this way I can send you from time to time an account of my life of retreat at Enghien.

And retreat it really is! No more telephones, metros, or meetings; in the last ten days, in fact since my arrival, I have only left the house once. I have two classes in the morning; apart from those I hardly ever leave my room except for the chapel, the refectory, or some other short proceeding; and in my room there are my books, my notes taken in the past, and all the problems that come quietly to the surface during the long hours of silence.

I arrived here on Sunday morning, and on Monday I started the course on grace, and the whole problem of the salvation of nonbelievers came back in a wave. On Tuesday I took up the treatise on creation, and there was the problem of the unity of the world; the same evening, before going to bed, I began my four days' reading of the book by Gross on the divinization of the Christian according to the Greek Fathers. This plunged me back into ideas that are very important to me; I found in it the elements for the study I have to finish between now and December on the Seal that is often mentioned in Scripture and the Fathers, and which seems to me more and more clearly to be the impress of God in us, the possessing of us by the Holy Ghost, that which marks every man with the love of the Father.

In this way we come to the whole discovery of the plan for the divinization of the world: the Christ God inserted into the very heart of mankind; mankind itself, as a single person with Him, slowly awakening in the course of ages (which in God's eyes lasts only as long as a smile, or the last step of a dance), slowly awakening to love, to the "image of God" that each man carries in his heart, and that mankind carries in its bowels.

I'm beginning this last scholastic year with a keener sense than ever of the solidarity that binds us all together in the same adventure, that forges our lives into one, and turns it into a moment, an act, a phase of the great human drama. There are plenty of things that baffle us and that we shall never understand on this earth; and things, too, that would revolt us if we didn't have, deeper than anything, our belief in love. . . . There's no solution for us to contribute except to give the utmost play to our lives, and dedicate ourselves to the human adventure according to the rules traced out for us by Christ: give, give, give again, and never stop.

You'll be thinking that I've left the earth! No, I say all that not because of the books I've been reading, but because of all of you, you whom I'm thinking about and from whom I've got such a heap of letters; I'm saying it because I feel the need to say it to myself, in order to find what possible answer there is to the multiple sufferings undergone by so many people around me and around you. As you know very well, our Christianity isn't just precepts and ceremonies; it's God's passion for this bloody world and the whole of squabbling mankind; it's the work of Christ who takes the love of all these poor men in charge, and it's a love that neither you nor I can judge, because God alone can read a human heart and see, perhaps, the greatest love when we see only defects and weaknesses. So let's leave the adding-up to God. His scales aren't the same as ours. All that's asked of us is to love mankind with passion, and show it that Christ's love burns.

With all my heart I offer my daily Mass, alone with Father G.—who is in the next room—so that you may be forever purified by a Christianity equal to your own selves and your surroundings. With you, I feel that I'm a small thing bound up with the world, capable of bringing to others, and getting from them, a little love and joy. God bless you. I am yours in Christ.

Enghien, December 20, 1946

Dear Friends. Just a line to wish you all the joy of Christmas. . . . I'm going into retreat on Sunday, and shall be coming out on December 31. I'm very pleased to be making this retreat. These two months of theology and silence have prepared me for it, but I still hardly know how to listen to the Holy Ghost. There are a whole lot of things I should say to you, but which I can't yet quite grasp. I shall be leaning on you during these days. As regards external life, I'm very much taken up with my studies. I've been putting together and typing out my little piece of work on the Seal of the Holy Ghost. I haven't finished yet; I'll still need a few days in January.

Now a piece of news. It's been decided that I'm to be in Paris next year and almost certainly to begin my life as a worker. You'll be delighted; I am, too. But more than anything I feel moved by the thought that I'll be giving the whole of my twenty years of study, traveling, experience, and training to the working class, with the determination to live with it, move to its pulse, and be truly bound up with it. . . . Please pray for that too. For my part, I'm not forgetting you; my best wishes, and my prayers, once again.

Enghien, February 24, 1947

My dear Friends. I am writing to you again for several reasons. First, because it's Lent, and the time of reflection and prayer, when we must work with the Church, in silence, recollection, and penance, for the resurrection at Easter. May humanity, in us, ferment under the Holy Ghost's action, may it be purified, may it grow in light and virtue. Then, I write to you all to save me from writing individually; I'm very short of time at the moment, as I have an exam at the end of June for which I have to work intensively.

Meanwhile, I'm still profiting by the silence and calm of this house, which allows me long days of study. I finished my little work on the Seal or imprint of the Holy Ghost on us, at the beginning of January. The texts of the Fathers on this subject are wonderfully rich, expressing all the grandeur, light, strength, and hope that lie in the Christian mystery, in the taking possession of man by God, in man's configuration with Christ, in our forward march under the Holy Ghost's guidance, so that we understand all the wealth and wonder of baptism, confirmation, and the other sacraments. All this needs to be expressed in twentieth-century language so that people of today may be nourished by it. With God's help we shall work together in the years ahead. I shan't be leaving here except to go to a conference at Brussels next week, where I want to show how the experience of Germany opened visions of a more community-centered and evangelical Christianity. In addition there's been a series of conferences here, putting increasing emphasis on the urgency of social problems: company reform, social insurance, trade unions, the international J.O.C., the attitude of employers; the situation seems to be getting more serious every day, and Christians are involved up to the hilt.

Thank you more than I can say for your letters, your prayers, and your friendship. You know that for me these mean the friendship and prayers of Christ's members, of Christ himself, and they make greater demands on me than the best resolutions. With God's help, you will make me do good—and God knows how many others you will help. In the experience of our friendship we'll discover what binds us—and all men—together; I am convinced we are only at the dawn of knowing these things. The strength and peace that we find in our prayers is one of the manifestations of Christ's spirit that is in us, that is between us, that fills the Church and makes her live, as it makes each of us live.

And yet, in reading your letters carefully, I have a feeling that several of you are struggling with all sorts of difficulties, or anyway with depression, whereas you should be pressing forward into a full spiritual life, borne onward by the light and breath of God, which are the presence within us of the Word and the Holy Ghost. We must manage to make the presence of the Trinity alive within us, let it light up and disclose undreamed-of possibilties of life and love. I wonder if you've read M. Grout's novel, Passage de l'homme? The man in question is a poor laborer who stops in a village one day, is first viewed with suspicion, and then delights the village (except the priest and the schoolmaster) with stories of the "Islands" where he's going one day, and where he'll take all the villagers. But the novel ends with the terrible disclosure that there aren't any Islands—in other words, there is no hope for man. For us, the revelation of love, of the love of the Father, through the Son, in the Holy Ghost, and the certainty of God's paternal presence at the heart of each man, of each home, of each people, of mankind—this revelation should be a source of constant joy and strength and trust; "good news" that fills us with delight. If we don't believe in it with our whole being (whatever the difficulties we have to contend with—physical and mental pain, temptation, sin), how can those around us know that the Gospel

is "good news" and that Christ has freed men from death
and sin?

I know all this isn't easy, but we've got to get there. "You
are the light of the world, and the light shines in the darkness." If everything is night and darkness around us, what
use is our Christian life? Obviously, as I said, it isn't easy;
it demands unremitting effort. It also demands the support
and counsel of the Church, from the sacraments and the
priest and from the group of Christians, the Christian "community," of which one can ask everything.

A priest's help is absolutely necessary—as the letters that
you write me prove—but it must be a priest who is always
at hand, who can be consulted at any time, about books,
about steps to be taken, about interior problems. You'll say
that you can't talk about these things to most priests, but
have you tried? At any rate, I maintain that it's absolutely
necessary, for me, for you, for every home. Don't be put
off by an initial failure; go on looking, and with the Holy
Ghost's help, you will find one. If necessary, don't hesitate
to shake them out of their administrative duties; talk to them
about your environment, and ask their advice on lots of
questions. The Church must become, in us, a real Mother
to whom people go for help and nourishment, so that we
can proclaim God to those who live around us. When we
have really discovered the richness and splendor of the
Christian life, our whole environment will be transformed
by it—first our family and then our friends, which is not too
easy! You should find, in the little Christian community that
surrounds you, the strength and peace of our friendship,
and much more besides. If the Christian life doesn't bring
you that, then it's not bringing its fruit, there's something
that has come unstuck, and you must find the crack through

which the fragrance is slipping away. Again I repeat—not in the interests of our selfish consolation, but in the interests of the witness that we must bring to the pagan world. . . .

God bless you. Pray for me, and for Annie, a young girl whose cure must be implored of Our Lady, and for all the babies who have just been born, and for the forthcoming marriages of Robert to Genevieve, and Jacques to Josette. And a special prayer for the summer camp of youth leaders that I'm organizing in Germany in July.

In the spring of 1947, Henri Perrin was engaged in working for his final exams and in organizing the international meeting referred to in the last letter. But his main concern was to become employed as a worker, for he felt that only factory life would enable him to understand the new needs of the mass of the population. But there seemed to be some question as to whether he would start this new life before or after his tertianship, as the following letter shows:

Enghien, May 7, 1947

Reverend Father. I would like to begin by apologizing for not having seen you at greater length in Easter week; but our first discussion had somewhat disconcerted me, and also I had a very heavy program of engagements already fixed for that week. So I decided to write you, but didn't hurry to do so because I wanted leisure to think things over. I have discussed the question with several people and regarded it from various points of view: with Father C. when he was staying here, and with Father R., who clarified many points. Then recently, Father N. brought information on the work Father L. is doing, and finally Father Rector summoned me yesterday to talk the matter over on your behalf.

Today, all I want to do is to set down simply what I think, as I hope to see you soon. I shall be in Paris on the 23rd (Friday); would it be possible for you to find time for me if I called between 5:30 and 7? The following day you will be taken up and I shall be very busy, as I'm coming for Jacques' wedding. I shall be leaving again on the evening of the 24th.

What strikes me immediately is that we don't see things from the same point of view. As you see it, "a team is to be launched in the proletarian environment, but this team must postpone its launching. . . ." As I see it, it's: "Tertianship or not? In agreement with Father Provincial and Father Rector, I would like to postpone my tertianship till later; therefore, let's get the team launched next year." Forgive me for formulating it like this, but that's more or less how it is.

As I said to Father Rector yesterday, personally I don't want to do my tertianship straightaway. Not only on grounds of the short time I've been in the Society, but above all because of the orientation it is desired that I should take. If I am supposed to do research on the paganized environment, I feel it is a golden opportunity, and one not to be missed, to have the benefit of those eight months of silence and retreat after several years of active work. I consider those months a necessity, in fact—for myself, first, because the experience will have sucked me dry and I shall need to clarify all the spiritual problems that will certainly have arisen; but also for others, for all those, whether priests or laymen, who are working in the same direction. You know better than I that it isn't so much a question of my own personal experiment as of the whole movement for working in the pagan environment. The mere possibility of being able to have in reserve that year of meditation becomes a necessity when I think of all those around me who would so love to have this privilege but are unable to. The question here seems to me quite different from that of a priest who is taking up duties along a well-marked-out road, and who can't easily be spared from his work for a whole year. . . .

I don't want to press the point, but there is a good deal more to be said about it. For instance, supposing the question of postponing my tertianship were decided, there would remain the problem of what I would do next year. Father Provincial thought of two years' teaching, to toughen me up, but he's now abandoned the idea, and I certainly don't want to press it. So there remains the alternative of going to work immediately in the pagan environment. You tell me that you've got nothing along those lines to propose at the moment. In that case, Father, perhaps you will allow me in all simplicity and filial duty to suggest several possibilities. As you know, I don't feel that it is tragic that I can't be incorporated right away into a team of the Michonneau type. I have a great admiration for their work, but I view it as only one among five or six possibilities for working in the missionary field. On the other hand, I recognize, with you, that it isn't wise to set out alone working in the heart of the masses, and anyway I don't want to.

And yet, perhaps you will allow me to submit some reflections here on the account given by Father R. on his activities last year. I think it is fair, but pessimistic, in the sense that it prejudges the future. There are plenty of ways for a priest to safeguard himself against loneliness and to find the support he needs. The companion a priest needs may well be another priest (in our case, not necessarily a Jesuit); or he may be a layman (as witness my socius Jacques); or he may draw support from the little Christian community he creates

around him. I don't feel that Georges had the experience of
this kind of support during his probation course as a worker,
for the time was too short and it wasn't known that he was a
priest. I think it would be easy to show that plenty of priests
who are now working among the masses are upheld by the
Christians living around them.

However this may be, I, personally, don't want to undergo
this experience immediately. But, Father, why not consider
the possibility of my beginning work while residing at the
Action Populaire? Of course there are drawbacks, but above
all there seem to me to be advantages. In this work with the
masses, which has got to feel its way before it finds the right
road, there is one thing which we need to guarantee, and
that is the link with Action Populaire. Why not begin there?
I think we are all agreed that we can only work in close association with you, if we want to work with the Society. But
this link needs forging. And furthermore, this work is bound
to take on a strongly social orientation and hence it needs
preparation in social problems that we lack and can't acquire
in mere after-dinner conversations. . . . But rest assured,
Father, that there would be no question of my being merely
nominally at Action Populaire and in fact spending my time
rushing right and left around Paris, going to meetings and
so on. If I've given ground for fears of this kind I regret it
keenly and apologize. Nothing is further from my thoughts.
My deep conviction is that our work can only be teamwork,
and I have in mind work with the Action Populaire (as
Father Loew works with Economie et Humanisme) and
with the team that we would eventually form in some working-class tenement.

So, in concrete terms, I would envisage next year as a
year of factory work, but in close liaison with Action Popu-

*laire. It is pointless to try at this moment to foresee exactly
how it would work out. I still have the idea I told you about
at the beginning of the year—of working as an electrician,
but not with the three months' trial I was envisaging then.
The end of September and October will be spent preparing
for the diploma in German that I must get this year. But
from November I would be free; and rest assured, completely
free, not pledged in advance as chaplain to some project or
group! Once we had really started, there would be plenty
of time for seeing what stages were necessary in the course
of a year....*

In August, 1947, Henri Perrin went to Maria-Laach for
the international Christian youth camp, and elsewhere for
other international meetings. He considered these to be of
very great importance, and on his return he wrote his impressions:

*The purpose of the meeting was to give the leaders of
Catholic Youth movements the opportunity of exchanging
ideas, although in fact very few top people were there. Instead there were militants and local and regional leaders,
except for one national delegate of the J.O.C.F. (for two
days) and the Belgian national leader of the J.E.C.F. There
were from thirty to thirty-five French, four Belgians, sixty
to seventy Germans, mostly students, as well as some representatives of Economie et Humanisme and of the Barbu
community. The Germans were interesting for their diver-
sity of origin—Berlin, Hamburg, Essen, Bonn, Heidelberg,
Mainz, and others from the French zone.*

*The organization (youth hostel for the girls, tents near
the abbey for the boys) was all that could be desired. The*

monks provided the meals with admirable devotion, and the abbey rooms are excellent for the conferences.

Information was exchanged concerning our respective movements, and there was discussion of Marxism, the social implications of Christianity, and national differences. I was very sorry that manual labor had to be abandoned, and also that there was so little study by small groups. The afternoons were taken over by general discussions which from the fourth day were led by the French. This arose from a lack of proper preparation, for which we were all to blame.

The result was an experience of astonishingly deep community in common prayer and a shared Christian life. The actual exchanges of view perhaps didn't go very deep, but at least contact was made. The Germans seemed not yet alive to social problems; they are inclined to see their Christianity as something purely interior, and even term as "activism" many things that seem to us as straightforward demands of the Christian vocation.

. . . Despite the brotherly friendship we experienced, and despite the genuine good will that inspired us, I retain from this and other meetings I had during the holidays with young Catholics the painful impression that many of these young people are, so to speak, branded with a kind of impotence. Many of them come from "comfortable families"—materially and morally (middle-class education)—and, for all their zeal and generosity, retain the imprint of a deep indifference, the indifference of people who don't have to fight against life. It is as if, because they "possess" the Truth (!) and a minimum of comfort in their living conditions, they have been established forever in quiet happiness. Their generosity appears as a virtue of perfection—praiseworthy, no doubt—rather than as a vital necessity, as it is for someone who has to pull himself and others out of destitution. The outcome seems to me a sort of impotence or spiritual infantilism. But I can't possibly blame these young Catholics for it; the responsibility lies with the Catholic backgrounds in which they were brought up. When I confided these impressions to Jacqueline Claudel she said: "I entirely agree . . . , but how can you change it without effectively taking the place of the one who has to fight against life? We have far too many safeguards." I think she's right. We must take their place! Alter alterius onera portate. It's from that moment that Christian witness begins.

After the Maria-Laach camp, I took part in other meetings, the two Lahr ones and the summer course at Tübingen University. The Lahr meetings brought together thirty Frenchmen and Germans, both writers and specialists in social questions. The first meeting was dominated by Emmanuel Mounier [founder and editor of Esprit] and the main writers of the Frankfurter Hefte: Kogon, Dirks, and Ida Görres, whose charity and humility won admiration. The second meeting was dominated by Folliet on the French side and Dr. Jostock on the German. Full reports are to appear in Dokumente (well known in Germany) and Documents, still not well known in France. I would like to underline how struck I was by what lay in common in the problems raised, and the identical reactions we found in the teams of French and German laymen. In practice, the only question raised was the social problem and the problem of Christians in the contemporary world. All those who took part were struck by the unanimity of views and feelings.

. . . Now we come to a few words about next year. As far as I am concerned, I am in full agreement with the plan sketched out at the close of the Maria-Laach camp: namely, that for three or four weeks there should be centers for the training of teams of workers. Each center would bring together some fifty-odd workers, 18 to 25 years old, with about half a dozen students and half a dozen workers who are active militants. These would not be religious camps in any confessional sense, but organized together with unions, tourist organizations, Youth Hostels, etc. The French administration is in entire agreement, and goes as far as envisaging free board for those taking part....

Although Henri Perrin was successful in the organization of Franco-German exchanges, which were anything but easy so soon after the war, his mind—as we can see by his writings —became more and more concentrated on the ideal of the priest-worker.

We find an instance of this in his reaction to an article by the Socialist writer, Pierre Hamp, on the subject of the priest-worker. In his article Hamp had written:

Even sincere Catholics are surprised at the delay in bringing the [priest-worker] activity into being. Nobody attends places of worship any longer, and church-sponsored charitable organizations do not attract young people. Of course, a certain respect for religious customs exists. The old virulent caricature of the priest is outmoded. Anticlericalism no longer finds a voice. Baptisms, first Communions, church marriages and funerals persist as family formalities. The parish is part of the proper thing, but not part of the soul. People no longer say "caw, caw" when the priest passes by.

But how explain the state of separation that is even more terrible than the open hostility that preceded it? The ecclesiastic does not even attract sarcasm. He belongs to a world of politeness and convention. Never before has his role been made so small. He is not even reviled; he is isolated, whereas he wants to move among the people. Custom has cut him off from work, just as the law has cut him off from the state.

Why does the Church find it impossible to penetrate the mass of the people? She no longer has adversaries such as Gambetta and his strong team of antipriests with their "Clericalism—that's the enemy!" On the contrary, she commands respect. And yet indifference in social religion is becoming greater than indifference in the religion of prayers. The most important activity remaining is the cult of sanctuaries, above all that of Saint Theresa of Lisieux, whose fashion is stronger than that of Bernadette of Lourdes. Why has the social force of the Church faded into nothingness?

Because it has not penetrated the world of the worker. Factories with 9,000 men have a dozen-odd Christian trade unionists and a few members of the J.O.C. The clergy is left preaching Rerum Novarum outside the factory, in parish associations and before industrialists. The union leaders are involved in the factory, and the priest is removed from it; he could only get in if he became a worker. No priest has dared to re-establish the primitive law of Christianity and go to work alongside those he wants to convince. No one has founded an order of priest-workers. The tradition of Jesus the Carpenter, of Paul the Carpetmaker, has no continuity in the padded upholstery of the Faubourg Saint-Antoine. The priest limits himself to his parliamentary role; he discourses. He doesn't do his day's work at the machines. With him, as with all those that insist on keeping their hands clean, the contempt for work shows not so much by words but by lack of contact. They praise work and keep away from it.

The priest does his military service as he is obliged to by law. He isn't recruited into the factory. Is it too late for this to happen? His place has been taken. Overalls would have helped more than the cassock if he wanted to incorporate the influence of a corporative Christ into the customs and ideas of people who work—not the pious nonsense of nursery tales, but brotherhood. . . . The separation between the Church and working life has been achieved by priests with clean hands, renegades from the religion of work, the religion in which the first disciples and Saint Paul were in communion. Trade unionists need to meditate on the virtue of preserving contact, their hearts set on the hope of salvation of society, but their hands at work. . . .

Henri Perrin was deeply impressed by this article, and in commenting on it he wrote:

How terrible that we are separate from the world, pitilessly cast aside into the ditches and pathways on the edge of the highways along which the masses march. Of course we had been told we were "apart," but we found it hard to believe, and hard to believe that the world cast us aside not with violence but, worse, with indifference.

We found it hard to believe that our churches were empty because the little stories we told and the little prayers we muttered "were no longer interesting." . . .

And then one day we emerged from the ghetto. You remember the marvelous pilgrimage of thousands of young people to Puy in August, 1942? That was a mere image or symbol of what a few months later was to be our life with the forced labor conscripts in Germany. And since that

*time, think how often we have come out into the daylight!
In this way we found* the world was in our hands. . . .

We have indicated how the book *France, Pays de Mission*
was fundamental for the priest-worker movement. Another
leader and pioneer, Father Loew, a Dominican who had
been a docker in Marseilles (and to whom Henri has already
referred several times in his writings), produced a book
about this time called *En Mission Proletarienne.** Henri
reviewed this book in the Jesuit periodical *Études:*

*Father Loew's book has long been awaited by everyone
who has heard of the "Marseilles brotherhood." It will be
read by all men of good will both within and without the
Church who think that the Church has still a word to say
to our contemporary world.*

*Father Loew writes, "After all, the time must come when
everyone will have to acknowledge certain hard facts." The
hard facts that leap from these pages can easily be listed: the
deep injustice of the condition of the workers, the tragic
situation of the "leaven" cut off from the "lump,"and the
need for a genuine religion of love. All this is quite clear, yet
hard to swallow, and hard to admit in practice because it
goes against what is accepted and demands that many in-
herited forms and practices should be abandoned in the interest of a genuine life of the Gospels.*

*The first hard fact, that of the injustice of the condition
of the working classes, lies at the foundation of the book. In
practice there are still plenty of Catholics who consider the
capitalist structure of our world to be just, and act as its
tranquil accomplices. But if it is proved that for a hundred
years capital has been living off labor and exploiting it in a*

* *Mission to the Poorest* (New York: Sheed & Ward, Inc., 1949).

hateful fashion, obviously every Christian worthy of the name has to say no to it. . . .

The second hard fact is that the leaven which should be intimately bound up with the bread is at present excluded from it. This can hardly be denied in view of the painful admission of thousands of priests in France and elsewhere. But here again the acknowledged fact is far from becoming a principle of action. The interest of the Marseilles experiment lies precisely in the fact that it has transferred itself into action. . . . "The contemporary masses ask the Church by what right she intervenes and claims to direct the spiritual and moral life of a people from above, without being involved with that people in all that concerns the daily details of its life and the daily earning of the family bread."

All this is tragic for the masses, who more than ever before unconsciously crave for Christ's revelation; and it is still more tragic for the priests. Wherein lies the solution for the priest and for the abandoned masses? Not in changing some petty detail of dress or habitat or way of speaking, though all these things play their part and call for meticulous revision; it lies in the humble, slow, and bold (bold, like the Incarnation) search for the community of life and destiny in which the priest will find his people. No single universal solution will be valid. In one place the search may lead to the formation of a group of priests as an apostolic team; in another place it will introduce the priest into the full community of work.

The third hard fact is that religion is essentially love and service of God and of men—nothing else. All readers will be struck by the wind of love that blows through this book. But here again there must be no assumption that love is born of pity "for the fate of the unfortunate classes." It is purely and simply what religion demands and expresses.

Religion, before being a ritual cult and, still more, before being a code, is a gift: It is the revelation and transmission of an overflowing and practical love. Without the love and the gift that make people into fellow beings and unite them in an inner way with each other, there is no religion, and the rites and the code are useless—worse, they are a scandal. Why is the proletariat "a pagan people with Christian superstitions"? Because it has never been loved. Efforts are made to preserve the rites and the code, but is real love extended to it?

To his Carmelite cousin

Dôle, September 23, 1947

My dear Sister. Pax Christi. I gather my silence has worried you. Am I right? And of course it's true that I haven't written to you for four or five months; but unless I'm wrong you owed me a letter. Anyhow, it doesn't matter. You must have heard my news from Mother; that I took my theology final in June, then periods in Germany, broken up by journeys between Germany and Paris. Finally, a few days at home, on the way to Dôle for my retreat.

At the moment I am in retreat and hence nearer to you than ever, and I'm on the eve of returning to Paris to go into a factory. Father Varillon of Lyons has been putting us through the Spiritual Exercises, and they have done me enormous good. The experience of these last few months has shown me once again, the hard way, how easily one gets emptied of prayer, of familiarity with God, and of contact with the Gospel; and how easy it is to waste time becoming attached to thousands of odd things.

I had to stop writing this letter because I found I had nothing to say. All I could discover in my heart was my weakness and sin and all the things which tempt me. Don't hold it against me, my dear Sister. If it results in my learning a lesson in humility and suffering, pray that this may mean that the passion and death of Our Lord dwells in me. At times I am very frightened of the months that lie ahead. I'm wrong about this, for I feel I'm not involved in them for personal reasons, but by the will of my Superiors, and with two other Jesuits, who will give me plenty of support. But I shall absolutely need to keep myself to a regime of prayer and recollection—and I know it will cost a lot to achieve this. In your letters you will have to ask me if I'm praying enough and whether I'm reading the Gospels and whether I'm meditating; and you will have to ask the Holy Ghost to keep me on the watch. The thought of your prayers is as dear to me as ever, and I have more and more need of them. Also please pray for a friend who is in prison and has to face his trial soon. Pray that all souls that come into contact with me shall force me to bring Jesus Christ to them. I feel confident that we'll manage it together, although with difficulty, and doubtless after silly mistakes on my part; but with God's help we shall be the means of bringing hearts to love Him.

While on retreat at Dôle, and on the eve of starting his new and exacting life, Henri made some notes on the problem of celibacy:

The celibacy of priests is incomprehensible, both as to theory and practice. In theory the priestly state does not belong to the natural law, like the state of marriage; and in practice the state of chastity is, naturally, almost impossible.

Anyone who does not accept the supernatural order may logically view the state of chastity as unlawful and even impossible.

[So he looks for its reasons]:

1. Witness to, and sign of, other values.
2. Sacrifice: I carry in my flesh the wounds of Christ.
3. The spiritual fatherhood of the priest.

I'm furious when I think of all the obscurity and darkness that surrounds the struggle for chastity in love and religious celibacy. When anyone is unfaithful to this, people accuse him and hold it as a grievance that he has infringed the moral law. Whereas they should say to him: "We needed your light, your testimony, and your struggle; we needed the radiance of your purity, of your love, of your voluntary chastity; we needed to discover the light of love, because love is God and the love of man is the sign of the love of God."

. . . Christ's love is a personal love and I have felt its burning touch. Who could give me greater love? How could I love someone with another love? It would be possible, but this is so much better. Christ tells me "to be with him in suffering"; for me, this sacrifice.

Weight of my body.

I've often met women with whom I would have loved to build my life, set out on the adventure of love. Often it has been at the price of a great wrench that I have let them go on their way, or that I have left them. But this wrench was necessary to give reality to my response to the love that weighs on me. Love has not been tested as long as one has not wished to suffer for the loved one. And then my love would wish to be the sign of another world, of other values, to which I have given my life. May it be my offering in the world of redemption, through suffering and the cross; participation in the mystery of the passion and the death of Christ.

It is not a question of the law of celibacy but of the vow of chastity, and I beseech You to accept this holocaust as a perfume of love.

Dôle, September 24, 1947

. . . If I have made a vow of chastity, if I am renouncing loving one woman, it is not only because the Church demands it of me, it is not only in order to imitate Christ; it is because I want to give the world another love, it is because I must reveal to the world all the Father's tenderness, all Christ's tenderness. Would this communication and revelation of Christ's tenderness to all those who suffer and wait be possible if I had given myself to a woman? I do not think so.

To have no other reason for being than to give joy, service, and help to all those I meet—that is well worth the sacrifice of my flesh. It is only in this way that I can transmit the fatherhood of the Father. The fatherhood which is love.

The Church has consigned the bleeding body of Christ to my hands. How can you imagine that I would have the heart to go and caress the body of a woman? The Church, after all, had the right to ask that of me.

. . . But if the Church asks this sacrifice of me, and if I have made this sacrifice, it was not to be separated from all of you, to have nothing in common with all that is dearest to you. I too am capable of loving a woman; I too am able to embrace. But I have renounced that embrace to be the living affirmation of the embrace of the Father for you. How can you expect me not to cry out if I see that you don't understand my sign, and if you are deaf and indifferent to

God's call? I bear Christ's bleeding body on behalf of distracted mankind, the sign of the Father's love and the pledge of his resurrection. That alone explains my celibacy, and that alone gives it significance in Christian eyes.

The following note, too, was written at Dôle:

A wife who is not yet a mother is a woman who has not created; she is, so to speak, in a state of expectation; and if her heart does not live for the child to come, it will easily be given to external things. A wife of this kind easily becomes "woman"—the woman who, despite a perfectly correct exterior, makes herself desirable to men in the most brutal way.

Once the wife has become a mother, she is no longer a woman; something has happened, a new world is born, and around her the air is no longer the same. This is never more noticeable than when we see a young mother leaning over the cradle and making her child smile. This woman no longer has anything fleshly about her; all she creates in men's hearts is an immense peace, real joy, an invitation to creation and song. Having watched her, we quietly withdraw, happy and strong and ready for all the tasks of man.

This new entrant into the world is so real that unless a man enters deeply into his fatherhood he runs the risk of finding the child a rival. Before the arrival of the child the home was two-dimensional, poised unstably upon the interplay of two loves and two egoisms. The child gives it its third dimension, its true proportion, consecrating it to heroism and throwing it into the most tremendous adventure.

V

Priest-Worker in Paris

(1947 –1950)

IT WAS finally decided how and where Henri Perrin should make his entry into working-class life: he would work in a factory in the *arrondissement* XIII, the quarter bounded by the avenue de l'Italie, the boulevard Massena, the Seine, and the boulevard de l'Hôpital. Already the Jesuits were beginning missionary work in this area, centered on the parish of Notre Dame de la Gare, and the idea was that the parish missionary work should be co-ordinated with the activities of the Jesuit priest-workers. Father R., Henri Perrin's first colleague, had already done factory work the previous year, and his report (referred to in Henri's letter, p. 83) on the religious and moral conditions of the workers had been pessimistic; but his experiences had helped to establish a pattern of life for the priest-workers. For instance, one day a week, Saturday, was to be devoted to spiritual relaxation at Vanves. The Communist question, which was later to present itself with such force, at this point seemed less important than

working out a true *situation* for the priest. The long letter
Henri wrote on the eve of his entry into the factory serves as
a suitable introduction to this chapter:

*My dear Father. You asked us to let you know our reflec-
tions and aims in the course of the year; herewith is a pre-
liminary account of mine.*

*. . . We are absolutely bound to work in all urgency at
preaching the Gospel to the dechristianized masses, but it is
equally indispensable that we should find out the causes of
this dechristianization. Of course there are materialism, ra-
tionalism, nonreligious schools, etc. But these are not
enough to explain why, within a century's span, nearly all
men have given up practicing their religion. . . . We have
been brought to a dead end, from which I feel sure God's
grace will redeem us, and we have to face up to this painful
fact in all sincerity.*

*Some of the causes lie in the past, and we can do nothing
about them, alas. Next year, the hundredth anniversary of
1848, will surely be a harsh reminder of the way in which the
Christians tragically abandoned the workers. It is becoming
more and more widely recognized that the great majority of
Catholics failed, and kept the silence of complicity, between
1848 and 1891 (that is to say, between the year of the Communist Manifesto and the year of Rerum Novarum), concerning the exploitation of the working class. And what have
we had since 1891 if not prudent silence and passive opposition to the Encyclicals? When Canon Belpaire of Brussels
was asked to take part in an international conference, at
Saint-Gall this January, of Social Christians from all countries, he wrote: "The doctrine of the Encyclicals is accepted*

unanimously, but practiced at a minimum, because of lack
of ability or, more likely, secret opposition. . . ."

But there are plenty of other causes for our present dead-
lock, and they have been bandied about to some extent everywhere: institutional sclerosis, sacramental ritualism, isolation of the clergy, etc. The outcome is the enormous gulf
that cuts us off from our contemporaries, especially those of
the working class. The proletarian world, the nonbelieving
world, has become as foreign and inaccessible to us as a
distant mission land; and, reciprocally, our religion is unin-
telligible to people who chance to enter into contact with
our institutions. . . . In a word, we need to strip ourselves of a
whole spirit of clericalism—a clericalism in opposition to
the Gospels.

The feeling of being at a dead end, the need for purification and interiorization and stripping ourselves of many-
headed clericalism, can be found in numbers of priests, both
young and old—as witness the documents that I append. I
call to mind a young parish priest in Paris, poor and loved by
his parishioners who are mostly workers and small tradesmen, who said to me three months ago: "In the last six years
I've done everything for my parish: I live poorly, my presbytery is open to all, and I know my people . . . and yet the
practice of religion is still falling off. Why?" Because the
forms of Christian life, taken as a whole, have become empty
of meaning for our contemporaries, because the Gospels are
no longer "good tidings," because the sacraments no longer
signify anything, because we have cut ourselves off from life.

That is why the presence of priests really living among
the masses seems to me a necessary condition of reform and
progress. . . . For, without knowing it, we seem at the moment like people struggling to keep their privileges. We turn

these privileges into rights of Christ, of the Church, and of truth, but in fact they are mere accidents, although ones it would be awkward to change. It is because we so often live in contact with a world where there is no suffering from capitalist injustice that it is vital for us to dive headlong into the life of the masses. . . . A lad of twenty-five, the son of a concierge in boulevard Haussmann [a fashionable street], who returned to the faith after a Lourdes pilgrimage, began looking for a priest with whom he could make contact. A few weeks later he told me: "Yes, I've looked, but you must realize, Father, that the priests here have more to do than busy themselves with workers like us; our district is full of countesses. . . ." Another priest told me he'd heard a priest with a parish of 25,000 inhabitants say, "The working people are dirt." Recently a Catholic professor wrote to Father X (I quote his exact words), "The worker is not fitted for religion." Personally I think exactly the reverse: I think the vast mass of our contemporaries are waiting for religion. . . .

[After suggesting some liturgical modifications adapted to the masses.] . . . People will say, Very well, but these adaptations call for caution and time, or they will lead to the worst deviations. And that is true, alas. But it remains that this development, in order to be possible, demands that the priest should be truly of his people, that he should be vitally familiar with their aspirations and their hidden life. Priests who are close to the people are absolutely indispensable for the service of the Church, clergy and faithful, so as to maintain contact, avoid sclerosis, and ceaselessly renew the evangelical and apostolic current. The principle of Leninism, formulated by Stalin, of constant reference to the people to ensure that one has not become removed from life and reality, to remain "in gear," is valid for all healthy societies, including religious society. . . .

One of the appended communications was from a young priest several months after his ordination:

Life goes on here, rather dully, with a sort of functionalization from which it is hard to escape even a little. . . . What is most dangerous for me at the moment is that I really have no liking for my life as a curate. A few isolated events apart (J.O.C. meetings, for example), my days are desperately empty. I wouldn't dare apply the word work to what we do in the course of a day: a marriage, an occasional funeral, catechism (three hours at the outside), and the church club. I also have the general hospital. There I have to face pagan suffering for the most part. I take books and cigarettes—I leave it to them to divide them up—and that stimulates some brotherly feeling in one ward (men). We get on well together. But as things stand, going any further seems impossible. When I leave I get the impression of being a hundred miles away from them all.

At last, in March, 1948, there comes the first direct news from *arrondissement* XIII.

6 Passage Perret, Paris, XIII

March 20, 1948

My dear friends. For some months I've been letting letters pile up, meaning to answer them some day with an account of the new life I've been leading for the past four months. I got back from Germany in September and worked until the end of December for a German exam. After that I joined

up with two priests already working and living in the rue
Jeanne d'Arc. The three of us form a team stemming from
the Action Populaire center at Vanves, with Father W.—
who drew up the whole project of our actual work—as Superior. He is following closely what we are doing.

One of us, Father S., spent three months working at
Citroën, during which he wrote his pamphlet A nous Chrétiens on the occasion of the strikes. This January he went off
to do a stint in the Moselle sawmills. He is thoroughly fit in
his new life, in spite of being 48, and in the months and years
ahead he will gradually penetrate a new world and analyze
it with the same passion he brings to the study of Valéry
and Bergson.

The other, Father R., whose companion in studies I was
last year and who has already had work experience in Paris
and Marseilles, started off with a job as assistant mechanic at
Say's big sugar refinery, which is almost next door to our
lodging. He had to lay off after two months because of sciatica, which has been troubling him for quite a while. At the
end of January he took up other work in the district (telephone parts). I tried to get into that factory, too, but was
turned down by the management when they found out that
I was a priest.

Of the three of us, Georges (Father R.), is by far the
most at home in the district and hence most in line with
our objectives. His factory—which is in the heart of the
quarter—and his contacts with various groups such as the
J.O.C.F. have enabled him to do a certain amount of spying-
out of the land. After a period of lodging separately for a
variety of reasons, we are both together again in 6 rue Perret.
We've been here a few weeks and are slowly settling down.

No. 6 is a little old house, and our room belonged to an

old dressmaker who went off to the hospital two years ago. The Fathers have whitewashed it and done it up with the help of Brother M. Its disadvantage is not so much that it has no water, gas, or electricity (although, thanks to Georges, we've had butagaz for the last ten days), as that it is situated in a wasteland behind the Say factory and is hence isolated. Our sole neighbors are three old women, a bistro, and a garage. It has become known that we are priests, and I think people are slowly getting some idea of what our mission is about. Every evening at 5:30 on my way back from work I drop in at the bistro to drink a glass of white wine and receive or make telephone calls.

I had to look around quite a while before finding a job. Now at last I've been taken on at a factory making insulating material and plastics (plates, bowls, radio sets, and so on). I began for the first ten days working as a molder, with two steam presses, on alternating shifts of 5 A.M. to 2 P.M., and 2 P.M. to 11 P.M. After that I was set working as a turner on a small series of standardized objects. The work was interesting and not very tiring, and even too calm, for its very nature isolated me. I am now with a small team of turners in a large workshop of women. Unlike other factories, it takes time to make contacts here because there is little talking. As it is piecework, and pay is low, the workers keep at it. Up till now my team workmates have refused to be on piecework.

Only very few people have gotten to know, from outside, that I'm a priest. In the factory itself, no one knows, and I have said nothing to anyone. For various reasons I decided to keep it quiet. First, for my own sake, in order to be in the simplest way one of them in their midst, to get into the rhythm of their lives, their thoughts, their way of seeing things. All kinds of things would have been different for me

in the last two months if they'd known that I was a priest.
And then if one says, without preparing the ground, that
one's a priest, there's a risk of setting up ready-made attitudes
of the kind people take toward the Church and the clergy.
A fortnight ago I thought the time had almost come for me
to say I was a priest, but I was dissuaded on two counts: it
was brought home to me how little we conceive of the distrust and resentment that have accumulated in people's
hearts against priests, and how little disposed they are to believe that we are disinterested.

I have a twofold aim. On the one hand to live as fully as
possible, and on the other to live as much as possible with
non-Christians. In practice my daily routine is very simple.
From 7 A.M. to 5 P.M. work at the factory. I get away at 5:30.
Then telephoning, the bistro, my mail, and one or two visits.
Toward 6:30 I say Mass in my room, either alone or with one
or two people present, unless I celebrate it in a group with
whom I am spending the evening. I hardly ever eat at home;
each evening I have at least one invitation, usually two.
There are a lot of meetings, with the parish clergy, with the
Paris Mission, with the Dominicans of 48 avenue d'Italie.
Every Friday we go back to Vanves for the evening and
Saturday morning: getting things straight, rest, prayer.

What are my main impressions? First—a strong and deep
one—that it is proper and necessary for a priest to be in this
factory as a plain workman. Then an impression that, following in the footsteps of others, I have entered a new world
which is unknown to the Church, a real mission field, a world
I need time to explore—months, years. Why do Christian
laymen never tell us how foreign the world we live side-by-
side with is to us? ...

Paris, March 22, 1948

My dear big Sister. I don't write much, but you mustn't
hold it against me. This letter will reach you with the joys of
Easter.

Thank you for your wishes of January 11. Pray that I shall
have a special fidelity to the Holy Ghost. For you I ask a deep
taste for God, with whom I feel I communicate in the mysterious life that binds us together.

All goes well, although on more than one point there is
something of a dark night. I often think of you and still con-
fide myself to you. Pax Christi. And I embrace you as a
brother.

I'm leaving on Thursday to spend the four days of Easter
in Germany.

It was about this time that Henri also became deeply involved with the Youth Hostel movement. His correspondence doesn't give a real impression of the part this youth
movement played in his life. It was for these young people
that he was granted permission for Sunday evening Mass—
the "campers Mass"—which took place at the Dominicans
of the avenue d'Italie. Sunday after Sunday he gave of his
best to these young companions of his, in expeditions, be-
fore-Mass discussions, the "campers Mass" itself. And they
were often joined by foreign visitors, especially Germans.
The years 1947–1950 meant the Youth Hostels to Henri
fully as much as they meant *arrondissement* XIII.

July 7, 1948

My dear Friends. It seems a long time since my March
letter. Like last time, I shall give you news of our team.

After his period in the Moselle, Father T. has been working at tarring on the streets of Paris. He does his day's work in six hours and goes back to Vanves in the early afternoon, so he is able to devote a number of hours to intellectual work. He's trying to join up with us again here, but it isn't easy, as much because of the housing situation as the difficulty of getting a job. Father R. has been going on with his telephone parts and with his penetration into the district, as well as assuring our liaison with the parish clergy and the Dominicans of avenue d'Italie. However, for the last fortnight he's been in the hospital with his sciatica; he's to have an operation, and then must take time off to convalesce. As for me, I couldn't get into Delahaye's motor works after Easter, so I stayed working in plastics, saying that I was a priest. I left the factory just now, on June 18.

When they heard I was a priest, my workmates had various reactions. By and large, the first was surprise, with some slight curiosity, but except in a few instances no problem arose. Some think I must be unfrocked, others that I'm there to earn my bread; some are reserved and show a cautious distrust, others feel sympathy because of the friendship that has already arisen between us. There were two groups with more defined reactions. The practicing Christians, members of the Christian Trade Unions, etc., joyfully welcomed the presence of a priest among them and viewed it as a grace; on the other hand, the C.G.T. and Communist element, except for a few militants who showed immediate sympathy, treated me with reserve and distrust for some time—a reaction that I found absolutely natural: we await actions before judging. Then at last the leaders shook my hand, gave me an opportunity to explain myself, and showed broad confidence, partly due to my attitude and what I said, partly because of refer-

ences to other priest-workers. With them, as with others, a
real friendship developed, a friendship which, had I wanted
it, would have led to my passing my evenings and my Sundays at Ivry, Vitry, and Villejuif. So it became rather difficult for me to leave the factory. But as staying on would have
involved going to Ivry, and as there was no question of my
leaving arrondissement XIII, I had to find another job in my
district.

More slowly than for Georges, but nevertheless surely,
arrondissement XIII is beginning to become my quarter. It
is a slow business because the quarter numbers more than
60,000, and one hardly lives in it for more than a few hours
a day. We are no longer living in rue du Chevaleret, as our
flat has been taken over by a homeless family. For the moment I've been taken in by André R.'s family, whom I knew
at the Agricultural School at Puy. As a way of penetrating
the life of the district, it's better than many an overture and
conversation. . . .

A few comrades in the district are going to take part in
the International Workers' Meetings in Germany. These
will follow the pattern of Maria-Laach, except that instead
of being just for Catholic Action militants, they will be for
militants of the workers' movement. They were begun by a
small group representing the different trends in the workers'
movement—various anarchist-communist syndicates. The
aim is to give militants among the workers, whatever their
tendencies, the chance of waking up to the international
workers' movement and hence of enriching their personalities in the struggle for the liberation of the proletariat. So
far the main groups represented are the anarchists and the
Christians. In spite of numbers of invitations and explana-
tions, the Communists do not seem very interested in the

project, either because they do not like the idea of meeting
with Germans, or because they see it as a means of forging
the Western anti-Russian bloc.

Taken all in all, these past months have marked the beginning of a slow penetration of the contemporary world,
with all that that implies of discoveries, difficulties, sufferings, and joys. Two facts have imposed themselves upon me
during the long weeks: the fact of the proletariat, and the
fact of unbelief.

After a month spent getting my bearings, my factory life
has been a slow and progressive revolt against the capitalist
world. This began with the inhuman attitude of the manager, who inspects the workers as if they were a roomful
of machines, and developed over questions of wages and
production, women's work, and the union struggle—and the
whole factory atmosphere in which workers have been
bullied and exploited for a century. Over and above my
personal reactions, I had those of the man on the ruling
machine who has had forty years of working life. He is a fine
type of skilled worker, conscientious, the sort of man I love
and admire every bit as much as a scientist or a statesman.
His conversation, which was infrequent, almost always em-
bodied the revolt that has slowly accumulated in the heart
of the working class. Whether because of the trivial fact that
he has no "right" to a snack between 7 in the morning and
midday, or because his time and the organization of his production are controlled, the worker has become alienated in
his work. He is not a man working with an engineer or a
manager, but a productive ability that has been hired and
has to be exploited to the maximum degree; he is not a man
responsible for what he produces, but a hand who is valued
only for his output. One of the most painful proofs of this

lies in the habitual raising of the targets of production without a comparable increase in pay. To this must be added the intransigent attitude of the employers toward the workers' organization, and the torpedoing of the workers' committees, at which the workers' delegates are fobbed off with tales about hygiene, while they are denied any say in the management. Add to this the fact that the firm, far from being a community of men working together, is not even guided by a human sense of production, but by a shameless desire for profit and money. Hence, so far as concerns the problem of capitalism, there can be no question of the education of the working classes, but only of justice and the proletariat's struggle for liberation. But to explain my ideas on this point I would need a lot more space and, no doubt, many more months of experience.

The second point that has been borne in on me is that of religious unbelief, awareness that the Christian message as it is officially presented is completely foreign to this world; at most it is an object of curiosity or a matter of history, but in no way an answer to the anxieties of our generation. The reasons for this rejection of Christianity have been stated so often that it is easy to review some of them here. No one accuses the Gospels—on the contrary, there is a certain feeling of nostalgia for them—but the Church is seen as a merely temporal, political power with a whole past of wealth and domination, and a concern with conserving its influence. "The Church is clever; it feels it has lost its influence; it is boldly making use of you to do a bad turn." The Church's activity is looked on as tactics, devoid of all genuinely spiritual motives. . . . All this, and plenty more, makes our Christianity seem as lacking in interest as Buddhism to the unbelieving world. . . . The genuine priests and genuine

Christians present in the modern world are still far too few, and far too lacking in holiness, and so the witness of their faith and hope, of their poverty and their love, is insufficient.

. . . To end, I shall quote these lines of a poem by Marcel, a twenty-five-year-old stevedore, which he recited to me by way of farewell when I left the factory:

But one day peace will reign on earth.
When all the peoples hold out their hands to one another,
There will be no more war.
Then on this earth, once steeped in blood,
We shall have joy in life, love and springtime.
From each nest,
Blessed songs will take flight.
O peoples, my brothers,
Unite, hold out your hands to each other,
Make war no longer.

Go with God for now. I entrust myself to your friendship and your prayers, and remain yours very fraternally in Christ.

P.S. I shall be in Germany from July 25 to August 20, then at Lyons until September 8. In the middle of September I shall be taking up work again in arrondissement XIII.

On December 5, 1948, Cardinal Suhard celebrated the golden jubilee of his ordination, in Notre Dame of Paris. On that occasion he said the following:

To save the souls of Paris, that is my first task.
It is for them that I shall have to answer on Judgment Day.
So you can imagine the anguish that I feel.

It's an obsession, a fixed idea that never leaves me.
When I'm in the suburbs full of somber factories,
  or in the brightly lit streets of the center,
  when I see that crowd, the elegant and the destitute,
  my heart is wrung in pain,
  and I don't have to look any further for the subject of my
  meditations.
It's always the same:
There is a wall that separates the Church from the people.
This wall must be felled at all costs
  to give back to Christ the crowd that has lost Him.
That is why we have been happy to entrust our
  Paris Mission to some of our priests, pioneers in the
  vanguard.

Paris, December 20, 1948

Very dear Friends. I am writing to you collectively; I really must give you some news—there are so many letters I have left unanswered.

First, I want to assure each and every one of you of my deep and loving communion at this Christmas time. I pray with all my heart that we may all be faithful to our vocation, which is to continue Christ's Incarnation and to make known, through our lives, his love and joy. I know it isn't easy, either for you or me. May our prayers bind us together and give us fidelity, during the whole of the coming year.

January 7, 1949

At last, after a fortnight, I'm going on with this letter. Since July there has been my stay in Germany and the meeting between German and French workers. We were

all delighted with it. Before returning to Paris I spent a
splendid fortnight in Lyons—at the Scolasticat at Fourvière.
I got back to my quarter in Paris on September 15 and
found a job a month later. But it didn't last long. After I
had worked three weeks in a little radio parts factory, I was
dismissed by the boss as a bad workman, with a week's pay
in advance. As a result, I had a long and violent argument
with my boss, who nearly hit me. I refused to be dismissed,
and this led to a second interview, with the works inspector.
In the end I gave way. But this shows the extent to which
the worker feels at the employer's mercy, and runs the risk of
being jobless from one day to the next.

Luckily I got taken on immediately by the Genève firm,
which has four workshops and factories in the quarter engaged in automobile construction. I am working in a pressed
steel team making wings for Ford trucks. Quite new work for
me, and I'm getting my hand in. Because of power cuts we
work only four days a week: Monday to Thursday, from 9
A.M. to 8 P.M. On those days I can't say evening Mass because there's a meeting every evening at 9. At the factory the
management and union leaders know I'm a priest, but no
one else. But they sense it, and I shall be telling them very
soon. The union gave me a first-class welcome and trusts me.
As I'm threatened with dismissal due to lack of work, the
union has asked me to do everything I can to stay. . . .

Regarding penetration into the life of the district, we are
keeping away from the environment of the parish even more
than last year, although we have brotherly relations with it.
Apart from meetings, which as far as I am concerned are
mainly with the young, we just have individual contacts
which are easily increased. To allow more frequent contacts
and to create our first instrument of culture in the quarter,

a team of us has started a film club which, in spite of initial difficulties, seems finally to be working. . . .

I won't go on. I just ask for your prayers more urgently than ever. You know you have mine. With my deepest friendship.

P.S. I've changed my lodgings four times. I think it would be safest to write to me c/o the presbytery, 24 rue Charcot.

Paris, March 31, 1949

Very dear Sister. Rereading the letter you wrote me on All Saints, I realize you had left me eight months without news. So I've taken my revenge! Don't worry about me. I have no problem about keeping in good health. I get normal food, and if I got overwhelmingly tired, I wouldn't wait to be told to rest. It's easy for us to give the impression of being saints, whereas endless mothers do with less food and sleep than us for their babies, so do husbands for their families, and comrades for their Party. My only problem is one of spiritual progress; not so much a problem of recollection (for the factory involves long hours of solitude and a certain recollection is possible in the noise of machines and work) as the problem of a total fidelity to the love of Our Lord, and hence to sacrifice. There are three positive things in my life at the moment that give it its orientation. First, a living faith in the Father's love for our humanity, and the vision of this new humanity in which Christ binds us all together (this vision is my nourishment, and I revert to it endlessly at our meetings). Then, human contacts, which I find even more demanding than the rules of religious life. I would say that contact with a living group of Christians and—equally, if not more—with groups of non-Christians (I am thinking particularly of the anarchists) is one of the things that gives our life as priests its greatest richness, grace, and strength. Then, finally, there is the Mass which is gradually becoming for me, as for the others, the fountainhead of the daily effort—through contact with the community in common prayer, through contact with the (universal) Church, through reading the word of God, and through the breaking of the Host. Imagine a Sunday evening Mass with campers of every kind praying round the altar—near-Communist militants, comrades who are looking toward anarchism, a Protestant pastor with his daughter, and so on. We are all united in human suffering, in man's dark night, in the universal predicament. . . .

I can't answer your letter any further. I feel I need a long conversation with you, for there are things we don't see in the same way. You can't conceive what it is to be a Christian outside the Christian ghetto (with its complacency, its traditionalism, its bogus problems, and—let's face it—its betrayals). Pray for a priest, a friend of mine, who wants to marry. But pray above all that the clergy and Christians should return to the Gospel; so many, so often, are so far from it. That's really all the world reproaches us with.

Till our next meeting. I must stop now. I give you a brotherly embrace and repeat once more my deep communion with you in prayer.

P.S. I have written a letter to the Cardinal on the subject of chastity. I'll send you a copy as soon as I find an extra.*

* The text of this letter to the Cardinal is lacking. But an acknowledgment from Archbishop's House says: "I am very grateful for the material you sent regarding the problem of chastity among priests engaged in your sort of work. You will find some of your phrases and conclusions reproduced in the document for which this information was required. This will tell you, better than a letter, of the Cardinal's gratitude."

Paris, November 19, 1949

Dear Baboulène. I see that Témoignage Chrétien has
organized a meeting for Tuesday concerning the trial of
Cardinal Mindszenty. Possibly because I am badly informed, possibly for other reasons, I must admit that I feel
no urge to attend it. More than that, I think if I went, it
would be to raise my voice in a way some people would find
surprising.

You and others doubtless have your reasons for protesting
against the way the trial was conducted. But I'm afraid that
many people—you may be an exception—lack the courage
to face what went before and what will come afterward,
things that a Christian worthy of the name nevertheless
should bear in mind. Theoretically, the way the trial was
conducted doubtless may be judged in itself; but in practice,
and in life, it cannot be dissociated from a historical context
which alone can determine the Christian attitude we should
adopt, however difficult.

I was in Budapest twelve years ago, discovering Europe
and beginning to discover "my country" (the West). I was
taken around by the president of the Christian University
Youth Movement. I had various contacts with the Hungarian clergy, and various glimpses into what we had better
call the Hungarian Church. I recall perfectly that this was
enough to make me say more than once to my friend, "But
do you and your priests realize that you are preparing the
way, and sooner rather than later, for one of those violent
reactions for which you should be the first to feel responsible?"

Moreover, to be exact about the business of the Cardinal,
even the enemies of Communism recognize that he was a
big landed proprietor in a people of serfs, and the active ally

of reaction (I was told yesterday that the reactionaries had the use of his estates for shooting practice). Certainly, many non-Christians, opposed to Communism, took a severe view of the attitude of the Hungarian Church, and of the Cardinal in particular. Only yesterday one of my friends was thunderstruck to learn (in his innocence he did not know it before) that a Cardinal of the Church could be a great landowner. The same people have harsh reserves about so-called Christian teaching in Hungary, and on the violent anti-Semitism fomented in that country by Christian society. How can you possibly dissociate the trial of Cardinal Mindszenty from the debit side weighing on Christendom, and especially on the Hungarian Church? How can you close your eyes to the fact that this has first and foremost to do with one of those many phases—and not, alas, the last—of the process of Christian compromise with the established order? It is a trial of this compromise, of the confusion between the "kingdom of God" and the "kingdom of this world." You know as well as I that we have to "roll back fifteen centuries of Church history."

This is what went before. Now for what comes afterward. Here again, you know as well as I the extent to which non-Christians and so-called Christians will exploit your attitude in the interests of a reaction which has nothing to do with the freedom of the Church. The temporal mirage still engages numberless so-called Christians. It is so much easier to protest (even justly) when there's an inner complicity more or less acknowledged, than to protest embracing the attitude called for by Christ—"Love your enemies, do good to those who persecute you." Do all you possibly can to get information as to the way the trial was conducted—which seemed iniquitous; but do it in full awareness of what a

truly Christian attitude requires of you. On this point I
don't think that having someone like Gide as a patron can
help you much. I was genuinely impressed by Gide when I
met him three years ago, but what earthly help can he be for
us when we have to adopt such a difficult Christian attitude?

This evening at my Mass I shall pray with all my heart,
with the Christian community, that we should learn how
to work humbly for the Kingdom of God, having the courage to confess our faults humbly and to love in the measure
that Christ loved. Fraternally yours in Christ.

The religious orders engaged in the Paris Mission (Capu-
cins, Dominicans, Franciscans, and Jesuits) held two days
of study in 1949, at which Henri Perrin gave the following
progress report:

We are not yet sure where we're going. We left the world
of security for that of insecurity, fully expecting a long
period of search. There are difficulties in arranging lodging.
For more than a year we have been without a proper pied-
à-terre. The team has difficulties resulting from deep differences in temperament, but regarding basic reactions we are
always in agreement. Difficulties, for myself, because of
instability of jobs (four or five in a year) and the dispersal
of my activities in organizational work—German meetings
and the film club. I have now become aware that all this
amounts to very little in thought and in life. An impression
of being all over the place. Clearest single experience that
of the Youth Hostel movement which at last recognized me
after a long wrangle to get rid of impressions of confession-
alism and proselytism. Difficulties with the parish mission
team, but close friendship and co-operation with the Do-

minicans of avenue d'Italie. Difficulties with the non-Christian militants owing to their distrust and reserve (perfectly natural). Grievous difficulties with employers. Employers, often themselves Christians, seem in reaction against the priest-workers, whose way of life linked them with non-Christian militants. . . .

Clamart, October 3, 1949

Feast of St. Theresa of Lisieux

My very dear Sister. My letters are few and far between, but the very fact of choosing this day to spend an hour with you is a sign that I'm not forgetting you and that you're always very close to me.

As you see, I'm carrying on with my life as a priest-worker. . . . Factory life is almost a secondary consideration, as what the Cardinal asked of us was to carry on an apostolate in the district.

At the beginning of the year, a team of Christians was slowly brought into being around me and a nun (in lay dress), who came to the district to work in the factory and work with me. In the course of this year she's worn herself out, however (overwork, too little sleep), and has gone off for the time being to teach in the school where she was before. So far the team is mainly composed of people from outside: for instance, a young woman doctor from Luxembourg who came to Paris to do her tuberculosis course; a young woman chemist who's bought a chemist shop in the heart of our district; a boy who came for three weeks, spent four months in a factory, and now works in the café—of which more presently. The team meets at least once a week for general discussion and Mass. There are two other teams of a similar type working in the district, with whom we are

in close contact; one formed around Father R., my colleague, and the other around a Dominican who lives near
and is also a worker. The aim of each of these groups is to go
to the people with humility, and to love this mass of 60,000
inhabitants. The ideal would be to achieve this slowly and
humbly, but you know how unsuited I am to that by
temperament. Is that good or bad? Anyway, it's a fact! A
year ago I started a film club, which is now entirely run by
the group. In the course of the year, in agreement with the
members of the team, we bought the "Café La Musette,"
a café and small dance hall, which we have turned into a
café-restaurant and meeting hall—the idea being to put this
hall (75 feet long) at the service of the district and so resolve for ourselves and others, too, the problem of where to
hold meetings. . . . My special job was to raise the money
for buying the place and doing it up; in six months we managed to raise more than 2 million francs on loan. . . .

All this must surprise you and seem very far from the
Kingdom of God. Above all coming from me, who never
stops saying that the witness of the Church is not spiritual
enough! It's true, and I'm well aware that it would take
pages to give any accurate description of our life; it's impossible to tell it, it has to be lived with us. But you must
realize that what we are doing is spiritual witness in the
sense that it is free from any sort of propaganda, and that
we are working in a brotherly spirit with all men, whatever
opinions they hold. There are two things that enable unbelievers to accept my witness: first, they feel that I am
extremely respectful of their consciences, and free from any
ulterior motive aimed at leading them to what they view
as the Catholic "bag of tricks"; second, they feel that I am
prepared to take over, to the limit of my capacity, the suf-

fering, the distress, and the "sin" of the world. On these two matters, at least, I feel I have been a true Christian and a priest of Christ.

I would like to go on to tell you about the social problem, which is of primary importance for us, and about the unavoidable contact with Communist circles, but I must stop for today or I shall miss my retreat, and you would have a right to be cross!

. . . The retreat ends on Saturday morning. In the cell next to mine our new Archbishop is preparing to take over his diocese next Saturday.* Pray for him too.

Go with God, my dear big Sister. I embrace you in a brotherly way and entrust myself to your prayers more than ever. If Mother saw this letter she would be jealous; she never gets as much!

Henri organized meetings of a day or, if possible, several days, to discuss progress in the district. The following agenda for a meeting of this kind, in the autumn of 1949, is typical:

Working Plan

Tuesday

What direction is our action in the district taking?
Is it a really co-ordinated action proper to the district, or are we dispersing our energies without a common bond?

Wednesday

The problem of forming a team that includes people who don't belong to the district or the working class?
Have we to some extent got inside the district?

* Cardinal Suhard had died on May 30, 1949.

Is this possible?
At what points have we got in?
To what extent?
And if we haven't, why?
How much must we live the life of workers? Possible eva-
sions.

Thursday

The part played by our Christianity—in the work we are
doing here, among ourselves, among others?
Stress the interior life and the witness of charity to be given
by our own lives and our lives together. Conflicts.
Means of deepening the interior life.

Friday

The part played by the priest: ought he to give up his work
or continue with it? His function in the team.
Spiritual and doctrinal formation to start out from the Bible
and the Fathers of the Church.
Health, sleep, and professional obligations must be assured.
Suggestion for the coming year's work: to see it in the con-
text of the Holy Year.

At the end of these few days, the missionary team defined its work as follows:

If we want our action to be more than a collection of activities without Christian significance or a guiding thread, it needs to be the manifestation and incarnation of something else; it needs to be the visible face of an inner spiritual reality.

This is the meaning of our work:

We want to make this district into one which fosters the union of everyone in the unity of Christ and their incorpora-

tion in his Body. Hence the need, on the human plane, of
everything that conduces to good will, union, and mutual
assistance. We want a just society in which people love one
another, because society is the human face of the mystical
Christ.

Hence the need to struggle against every form of injustice,
the great social and individual sin.

We want to be the continuation of Christ, both as individuals and as a community, to let Christ shine through us
and to make our community the reflection of the community of the Trinity: union and love.

We want to be witnesses. Hence we must live an integral
life of charity, the keystone of everything. Individual and
collective dedication.

Our activities will be our way of showing that our love of
others and our will for justice are more than empty words.

In writing to his Carmelite cousin in October, Henri had
referred to the problem arising from "unavoidable contacts
with Communists." There is an important historical background to these words.

On July 1, 1949, the Holy Office issued the well-known
decree condemning Catholics who either belonged to, or
collaborated with, the Communist Party. And on September 8, the French Cardinals published a letter, stressing
that a religious rather than a political meaning was to be
given to this decree. The militant Christians of *arrondissement* XIII, working around Henri and the other priest-
workers, were deeply disturbed. The condemnation was so
severe that it set them wondering about the authenticity of
their activity. Throughout the summer there were meetings,
conversations, consultations, in which they tried to recon-

cile their position at the heart of the Church with their position regarding Communists and Communism. The torment
that Henri, with others, was to endure for the next five years
foreshadowed the ultimate priest-worker crisis.

Were they "favoring in any way" the advance of Communism by working side by side with Party members or by
adopting Marxist methods of analysis?

Monsignor Baussart made an appeasing statement in the
Semaine Religieuse: "Numbers of people may be worried
by the fear that this decree favors a political and social
point of view opposed to the interests of the working classes.
Some have said as much. What this text condemns is the
materialist and anti-Christian doctrines of the Communists
—it says so expressly—*and not the social reforms which
need not be attached to this doctrine,* as the Popes have
abundantly shown in their Encyclicals and allocutions."

The following reflections express the suffering of Christian working-class militants:

1. Even if the Holy Office decree is not political *in intention,* it is political *in effect;* of the two political camps
confronting one another in the world, one is strengthened
by it, the other weakened.

2. "In practice, a militant who has become engaged in
the social struggle and finds himself simultaneously a Christian and a Communist (which of the two he was first, is
irrelevant), though he may have given up lucrative and
reputable work to become poor among the poor and help
to improve conditions of work—this man is now in a position of bad conscience and might even be refused the
sacraments. On the other hand, the irresponsible factory
owner who underpays his men, the slick speculator, the big
industrialist who cheerfully strangles his rivals—these may

approach the Holy Table to receive the Body of Christ without batting an eyelash." (A priest-worker)

3. "Efforts to dissociate the working class from Communism are largely an abstraction. Whether for good or bad, Communism is the main expression of the working class in its forward march. A decision against Communism is, in fact, interpreted as a decision against the poor and struggling classes." (Father Bigo, at Lille)

4. "At the works, what does the Church represent by way of hope for our comrades? Nothing. What does the Communist trade union delegate represent? Everything." (A priest-worker)

Henri Perrin himself wrote:

I feel more and more the parallel between our time and that of the collapse of the Roman Empire under barbarian pressure. It is not a government which is in process of collapsing but the whole civilization of capitalism, which is built on the freedom of profits. It is collapsing because of its excesses—trusts, high finance, the loathsome selfishness of the rich. On the other side, there is the upsurge of the proletariat, bent on creating a new order. Much more even than at the time of the Roman Empire, the Church seems to be bound up with the established order.

In the fourth century the Church had to baptize the barbarians. She must now baptize Communism. But this is a very different matter. The barbarians were no more than a brutal force that had to be dominated, raised up, and made human. Communism is a mystical doctrine whose inadequacy we must make felt. The barbarians had no rights over the spoils of Rome. The workers have rights over the spoils of capitalism, which they built with the sweat of their brows. . . .

On January 6, 1950, there was a day's conference for the priest-workers of the Paris Mission. These were the lines of research proposed:

The need to be a community faithful to the mission which has been confided to the priest-workers.

The need to be sharply aware that we are priests on a mission (not a special type of curate or Catholic Action chaplain), and hence must be ready for all the ruptures that this situation may demand (by very definition, a missionary comes into contact with a world that is foreign to the Christian world).

Awareness that we are a community set apart for a precise mission, that is to say, unattached to the ecclesiastical world of the Church in a Christian country.

Awareness that we are a community attached to what is poorest in the world, concerned to keep disengaged in order to attach ourselves to those in need.

Convince ourselves that the influence of the priest will be in inverse ratio to his rank.

Acceptance of the necessary ruptures. We must not be of the clergy, of the Catholic world, of a religious order first and foremost, but of the workers' world in its suffering.

The need to take the extreme position in the world that has become ours; no going back to our past, no taking up with past education, past environment (a temptation in our frequent loneliness).

Need to study the position of the Mission vis-à-vis the parish, Catholic Action, and the Communist world.

*Need to reflect on our priesthood in the light of our
commitment to the workers' world.*

*N.B. These are mere notes for which I alone bear the
responsibility. Henri Perrin.*

In March, 1950, a great wave of strikes for the readjustment of wages spread through France. In *arrondissement*
XIII, the presence of so many militants, with various em-
ployments and strong links with the parishes, put the parish
priests and their curates into the position of actively sup-
porting the committees set up to help the strikers. And a
poster entitled *Justice*, signed by all sorts of people including Christians and priests, was put up. It said: "The strike
is just and legitimate. Authoritative voices of every point of
view have said so. The employers' indifference to the workers' obvious needs, their concerted refusal to negotiate,
their desire for profits before everything, all are prolonging
a dispute which will have deep repercussions on the life of
our country. The Goverment, by intervening in a strike
voted democratically and justified by suffering, has incurred
heavy responsibility. The use of radio, of credits from the
Bank of France, and of the police on the side of employers,
has encouraged them in their stubbornness. . . ."

Henri Perrin wrote personally to the M.R.P. (the Catholic Party) deputy in his constituency:

Paris, March 2, 1950

To M. Cayeux, M.R.P. deputy

*My dear Friend. I feel bound to write to you in view of
the way the situation is developing over our strike. I have
been playing an active part in the strike since February 22,
and am trying to get further information on the situation*

at the regional and interunion level. I would like to tell you how just, necessary, and strictly professional in its origins and development I consider this strike to be. Any statement to the contrary would appear to a participant in the strike as mere lack of information or bad faith. To speak of a "political strike" is an odious calumny.

In this strike I accuse the employers. I accuse them for refusing the wage increase demanded last autumn by certain sections of industry. I accuse them for not having prepared for the unfreezing of wages, while always taking refuge behind the Government umbrella. I accuse them of torpedoing the development of workers' committees, which were the only faint hope of redressing the situation between employers and workers. I accuse them of evasion on numerous occasions since the beginning of their talks with the metalworkers' union, although readjustment of wages appeared necessary and urgent to everyone. I accuse them of bad faith in the way they negotiated the talks, in the arguments they used, and in their use of information concerning the strike. For all these reasons, the attitude of the employers, which keeps workers' families in need and forces the workers into a condition of revolt, seems to me strictly criminal. May I repeat and underline the word: criminal.

Given this situation, I am amazed by the attitude of the Government, which, instead of respecting the free play of the forces of workers and management brought about by the unfreezing of wages, is trying to break the strikes by instructions and support given to the employers. If the Government is afraid that the strike may be used for political reasons—that is to say, against the unloading of American arms in mid-March—the best and only way to avert such a development is to put pressure on employers for immediate agreement on the 3,000 francs, which will automatically result in a return to work (whatever the employers say). The attitude of the Government shows deep ignorance of everything that is happening in the workers' world.

Please do not hold the position I have taken against me, for I believe it to be necessary. And please believe me to be still cordially yours, H. Perrin, priest-worker, metalworker.

The activities of 1950 culminated, before the summer holiday, in a wonderful retreat, when the whole missionary team gathered around Father Perrin and his colleague.

VI

Tertianship

(1950 – 1951)

HENRI PERRIN passed his third year, or tertianship, at Ineuil, near Chateauneuf du Cher. He went there in September, 1950. His departure from active work, and from the center at 151 boulevard de la Gare, was a great loss to his countless friends, as the letters he received show: "Your departure has left a terrible gap." "You've done so much for our Youth Hostels." "So many other fellows were hoping to meet you." "You made me understand and love the Church; before I met you I couldn't take it." "We miss you terribly. Naturally *we* do, but it's even worse for the fellows coming from the Scouts, who seem quite lost in face of contemporary problems, question everything, and fall into Marxism." ". . . The broad vision of the Church that you've been giving us these last two years and which has been for me personally not only peace and consolation, but a spur."

Ineuil, September 26, 1950

My dear big Sister. I can't remember how long it is since
I wrote to you, but it must be months and months. Please
forgive me—I ought to have found time, but the months
have flown by. And then I knew that once I had left my
overactive life in Paris and gained the silence of my tertianship I would be able to write to you. And here I am.

I have never forgotten you, and I count on you more than
ever before. In a week I'm going to start my thirty days'
retreat. I know that you will always be beside me and that
you will help me to find Christ and lose myself in Him and
in the great silence. Then later I shall be able to read
Theresa of Avila and John of the Cross at my leisure. That
will be like having a dialogue with you. And of course I shall
give you all my impressions.

As Mother may have written you, I left Paris on September 9. I thank Christ for my three years of working-class
life. Both in the factory and in the district, the affection
and trust of my friends and of people generally seem to me
more and more, as it were, a manifestation and reflection of
the Father. It would take too long to tell you about all this
in detail. Suffice it to say that I am even more convinced of
the absolute necessity of priest-workers in the Church, and,
if it pleases God and my Superiors, I shall be taking the
work up again next year.

In your letter of June 18 you used a phrase that I would
subscribe to with my whole heart: "Perhaps we think too
much about perfecting ourselves instead of trying first and
foremost to love." Am I too inclined to make that my
motto? I don't know, but I do know that it would be a good
definition of these last three years. I have tried before every-

thing to be faithful to love, the love that has spurred me on through the long days, and in many different forms; but this love has often been very hard to bear, bringing with it as it does the sufferings and the sin of others, as well as my own. Sometimes, at the end of the week, I felt I just couldn't go on, with so much suffering and despair to share in. It was then that I rejoined you at my Mass, and rested on you for support, for you too are, for me, the Church and Christ. You must realize, Lucie, that in these three years there have been many acts of weakness, hesitation, and cowardice; but there's also been a descent into poverty and love, a poverty of the heart and a response to the claims of love, which, in my belief, are the richest gifts Our Lord has given me and which I could never lose in any circumstances: and those, I hope, have redeemed me. Please thank Christ with me during this retreat.

Yes, I saw Mother, as she probably told you; but in all the turmoil of my life in Paris I couldn't have a proper talk with her such as she would have liked. She felt badly about this. A month later I also saw Andrée and Pierre, and before I came here I was able to spend five days with them and see the children, who have grown a lot. So far they've had no real difficulties with the children, except with François and Marie-France (the two eldest), and also, I gathered, with Etienne, the fifth, whom I didn't see. I'll do everything I can to back up Andrée in the years to come because, with Pierre alone, she wouldn't be able to guarantee the upbringing of all her little flock.

I will read the two articles in La Vie Spirituelle that you mention, and tell you what I think of them. At the moment I'm busy with the Apocalypse, which I have wanted to explore for a long time. I'm also rediscovering the Psalms, which I wish you could recite in French; it's much more nourishing.

Finally I entrust my tertianship to your prayers, as well as the team I have left behind in Paris; also two special intentions that I have very much at heart—both SOS's.

Go with God. I'll be waiting for a letter. I pray for you, and count on you, and embrace you fraternally.

P.S. If you've got any advice to give me regarding spiritual reading, I would be grateful. We get the Études Carmelitennes. And please be my guide in reading St. Theresa.

Henri Perrin's mother wrote to the Carmelite at much the same time:

November 29, 1950

. . . Has he talked to you about going to Russia? And when? I haven't any details and I don't like asking him, I don't know why; yes, it's because I don't want to show him that I'm consenting to its happening. And yet, dearest Lucie, I can't go against him in this. It would be going against God's will, if Henri has made up his mind; and then I wouldn't like to make him lose a higher crown in heaven. But accepting a thing like that is hard.

Yesterday I got a letter from him in which he said that he has taken up his notebooks that he put aside three years ago, and that he has made his will and wants his notebooks to be given to me should he die before me! Tears kept coming into my eyes all yesterday afternoon, and I felt a tightness at my heart. . . .

To Paul E. (A Youth Hostel colleague who was ill)

Paul, now that I've left Paris for ten months' silence and solitude, I feel more at ease, and here I am with the same deep friendship as ever and the same prayers which I have never neglected to say.

There were two main things worrying you: the attitude to take to illness, and the attitude to take to love. Regarding illness, you mention B. as an example. Here, for you to ponder over, is a passage from the last letter I had from him: "My health is getting worse, and I'm going to have to give up most of my activities in the Ligue, except fellow feeling or solidarity. And that's as much a part of our lives as air and bread." My dear Paul, above everything we have to love the Father enough to leave things to Him. I would give anything to see you freed from the anxiety that's gnawing you. It's quite simple: the principle is that Christ wants you to get better and hence expresses his will through the doctor. If He is calling you to some other vocation, He'll show it to you all in good time without your having to worry your head about it. All you have to do is love Him and offer Him your days. He'll do the rest. It follows that you can't have any outside "activity" except what prudence dictates. And don't try to make a decision about this yourself; put it into the hands of someone else—the doctor, or a nurse you trust, or a friend who knows all about you. You don't seem really convinced that your activity as an invalid can serve better than the exterior activity you're longing for. I'm going to quote from another letter I've just received from a friend who has given her life to the Mission and has just come back to Paris with a double cancer. She is condemned to death, and says:

"I'm happy in spite of everything. I'd been afraid of this illness, feeling it coming. Now that it's here, I see it as a gift of love. Yesterday's Mass and your letter have given me this full view of faith and are helping me to live it (I should have said: us). I was hoping it would be like this, or rather I didn't even dare to hope it. . . ."

Paul, your illness is like my present solitude. What's the point of my being away from Paris for ten months when there's so much to be done there? If I'd judged merely by appearances, I'd have stayed on.

And now, the attitude to love. I sympathize with your impatience. But there again, Paul, we have to put things with serene trust into the hands of the Father. In any case, you will know love, you are intended for it, whether it comes through the love of a woman or in some other way. And when I say that, I'm not trying to delude you. It's we who get deluded about love; we look for it, and don't know how to look for it; we ask it from a woman, who perhaps isn't the one who will lead us toward love. You see, Paul, love is God, and it's Him we are seeking through a woman, as through everything else. It's one of a Christian's riches to know that.

Speaking practically, here again, here more than ever, any serious step has to be subordinated to your getting better. Waiting will be hard at times, but you just have to wait. In this, too, you've got to believe that waiting is a richness in itself, and an increased proof of love.

In two days' time I shall be burying myself in the silence of the long thirty days' retreat. Help me by praying for me. Be faithful to me, as I would like to be to you. If you've got a Bible, read a psalm slowly from time to time, and so make

the prayer of all mankind pass into you. You'll find it works.
Go with God. I embrace you fraternally.

From his notebooks

October 30, 1950
. . .To penetrate into the mystery of the cross, I must rediscover all the weight of suffering and sin that overwhelmed
me in Paris.

The weight of the sin of the world, with all its secretions
of pride, hatred, and contempt; with all its dissensions, dis-
cords, life-and-death struggles, and death; sin proliferating
from generation to generation in the heart of mankind; sin
that affects us all and lays us all low at one time or another;
sin in which we are all interlinked, I dragging in others,
others dragging in me; mankind's great Yes to self-idolatry
and the rejection of God.

The need to understand that man would never have
emerged from it without Christ. Man would have recoiled
before the great sacrifice of renouncing self, and choosing
God; he had recoiled. God Himself, by making Himself one
of us, by making Himself man, had to retrace the path in
the opposite direction, reopen the passage toward God,
make the sacrifice.

But that had to be done at the price of His life, through
death. He who loses his life shall gain it. In Christ all the
aspirations of mankind, all our hours of hope, all our efforts
to resist evil, all our sacrifices (it is more apparent than ever
that henceforth we must never envisage anything save
through the cross) find their way and their fulfillment. The
meaning of the unique sacrifice, which fulfills all things,
through death.

Reread Isaias 53.

Reread *Epistle to the Hebrews.*

Two other letters from the period of silence during his tertianship:

To Paul E.

Ineuil, November 22, 1950

My dear Paul. I have your two letters of October 11 and November 7. Thanks. I think Christ is drawing you slowly to Him and that you are gradually finding peace. Your final words, "To remain open to all things, to love what comes, to love in silence and without ostentation," show your progress. In spite of appearances, you are nearer everything and everyone the more illness plunges you into solitude. Cherish like a blessing the memory of all your friends of the Youth Hostel movement, and of Monette in particular, and particularly if she is never to be yours. Let things be; Our Lord is guiding the ship, and He will give you over and beyond what you seek.

You ask advice about the commitment of young married couples. There was recently a series of articles on the subject in Témoignage Chrétien. They might help to clear your mind. Personally, I don't think there's any need to worry too much in advance, and still less to work out in advance what you will be able to give away. Many pagans don't do this, and I think it would be anti-Christian if we did. A little trust in providence please—even a lot. The Gospels contain expressions that leave no doubt about what we should do: "If someone asks you for your coat, give him also your cloak." To those (whether Christians or non-Christians) who have enough faith to remain always ready and welcoming, Christ will always give what is necessary—and generously, I'm sure. I don't believe in too much provision for the future, but I do believe in imagination and astuteness. When we open our door, other doors open. Unless Our Lord has a period of trial in reserve, but in that case He gives us the wherewithal to face it. My friends were reading Le Devoir de l'Imprévoyance ["The Duty of not Providing for the Future"] by Isabelle Rivière; I haven't read it, but it seems to be useful.

As for joy, you'll experience this, insofar as you experience peace. I understand very well what you say about your attitude to Monette. However hard it seems, say the prayer of Father de Grandmaison: "Virgin Mary, give me a gentle and humble heart so that I may love without asking anything in return." You've got to find peace on this point, too.

Go with God. I am in communion with you and embrace you fraternally.

P.S. Have you a Bible? Read a psalm from time to time, and the last two chapters of the Apocalypse.

To his friend, Paul G.

Ineuil, November 29, 1950
. . . What's my news? My silence cure proceeds, efficacious and fruitful. Not always easy; I need the spur of so many friendships to keep me ceaselessly in the presence of the Lord. Have I lost ground? Or is it on the contrary a deepening of "docility" to the Holy Ghost? It appears that abandoning myself to the will of the Father is something much more demanding, constraining, subtle, than I imagined it

in the past. That's one aspect of the problem. The other aspect, and the object of my constant meditation, is my pre-occupation with the last three years, with the zest for life side by side with the world God is making, with mankind on its sorrowful pilgrimage, with a Church in which I see more and more the pre-Resurrection Christ—whereas before, in my life "apart," I'd seen it as glorious (though with an adulterated glory). I ponder the Apocalypse, but it's long in coming. Pray to the Holy Ghost for me.

For the rest, I'm leading an extremely quiet life in a château (of course!) in the Bas-Berry, in a countryside that's slowly dying, like many other corners of France. I have two recreations, chopping wood and chatting with my companions (a fine lot). Oh, yes, for the past three weeks I've had a guitar! And then, mum's the word, I'm thoroughly enjoying reading Trotsky. There's a real giant that you've produced. I get the idea that the people who are now crying shame on Stalin's Communism would surely have raised a similar outcry against the Bolsheviks in 1917. Wouldn't they? I would like to know Trotsky's views on Stalin's Communism. Where could I find them?

What's new in Paris? From here you get the impression of a colossal machine which goes on working through thick and thin by virtue of the wealth acquired. And always more or less fleecing the underdog. What a muddle!

I'm thinking of your children. When they leave Paris for the atmosphere of home, it must seem a change of worlds every evening. If Marguerite can think of any important advice to give my sister about the religious upbringing of her eight kids, please let me know.

Till our next meeting. In communion through prayer,

with all mankind, which is, in spite of everything, the Body of Christ.

To his Carmelite cousin

Ineuil, December 21, 1950

My very dear Sister. Thank you for your letter and prayers. They are working. In the last three months Christ has been slowly drawing me toward Him. And I'm now happy to say that your great saints have helped a lot; I've read Louis Bertrand's life of St. Theresa, and, more important, I've read one book on St. John of the Cross by the Carmelite Father Bruno. This book did me a great deal of good. John of the Cross is a giant of love and penance. Poor as I am, I love him truly and have decided to read some of his works in January, as well as those of Theresa. Your prayers will guide me and make my reading yield fruit. There's not much to tell you about my life here, unless I told you everything, and that would take reams.

I'd prefer to take up one or two points in your letter. Don't worry; I don't think going to the altar has become a "habit." I've even made making the sign of the cross not a "habit." The Curé d'Ars said that "if the priest understood himself, he would die." But it is just as true to say that if men understood themselves (as sons of God and as the Body of Christ), they would die. Remember the many mystics who thought they were dying when experiencing the burning of divine love. I wish people would understand that the real gulf is not between priests and men, but between a mankind that has received no call (it doesn't exist) and the divine vocation of the human race. The Bible never speaks of priests, but often speaks of "the holy people and its royal priesthood." In this there lies a whole vein of theology and spirituality from which very few draw nourishment, in spite of the efforts made by some.

You also say that our world is engulfed in error, selfishness, and hatred because it has turned its back on God. Yes, since original sin. And yet, since that time—a time we find very mysterious—the world has always had a God: the Word which creates it and gives it life from within, and which, binding up all humanity with the humanity of Christ, slowly stakes out the landmarks of the Incarnation and sets mankind on the path toward the greatest sanctity. Our present world, like every epoch of human history, consists of darkness and sin and death wrestling with God, yet it is mankind on the march, opening itself out to light, holiness, and life. It's up to us to be able to perceive the signs and recognize the hand of God.

. . . I must stop now to catch the post. I remain your brother in Our Lord, and in the friendship of our great saints.

P.S. The matters that I recommended to your prayers seem to be working out well. Thank you.

During this period, Henri Perrin gave two talks to his fellow Jesuits doing their tertianship, on the subject of the priest-workers and the isolation of the Church from the working classes. These talks followed the lines of thought he had already developed at study week ends referred to in Chapter 5.

On January 1, 1951, Henri's friend, Paul G., wrote him a letter in which he reverted to calling him "vous" instead of "tu," as being more suitable when addressing a priest. He also said:

The way things are going makes it look as though our lives are going to be short, and the more enormous and immoderate the problems become, the more man's actions need to be well-judged, precise, and rigorous to face the storm. I have come to the conclusion that we should now live in an eschatological climate, the only one in which the Christian can live. Events are out of our grasp, but not immediate contacts with men. War, in bringing us nameless miseries (against which we must fight to the very end), will perhaps also bring us that poverty and that sense of justice and brotherhood which we have completely forgotten and whose exercise is perhaps made impossible by the present state of society.

I am surrounded by families that are breaking up, by people who seem to be yielding to an inner softness, to a sort of intoxication of self-destruction—it's a real decay in society in which the life values are carried forward only by Christianity and Communism. But what a gap there is between them! Christians are beginning to realize that Communism, in the form in which it is presented to us, entails risks we cannot accept, and gaps and denials we cannot accept, either.

You are lucky to have this time for thinking things over. I repeat, you are lucky. Profit from it to the maximum. You will need so much rightness of judgment, solidity, and peace in the midst of the men you are going to rejoin.

Let's look after our health; in this sick world, it is a benefit of primary importance to offer to others. . . .

Ineuil, January 8, 1951

My dear Paul. Thank you for your long letter. All right, I revert to "vous" with no difficulty or regret, believe me. . . .

I understand your point of view and agree with it entirely, except what you say on the sacred character of the priest. Not that I find your idea excessive, but it seems to me that it doesn't sufficiently take into account the vision and awareness of a whole world that is consecrated, of a whole mankind that has been baptized and is God's child. The priesthood, far from belonging to us, is delegated to us by the Body of Christ, which is the whole Christian community, of which you are a member. The whole universe is sacred from the fact that it finds its unity in Christ and bathes in the grace of the Holy Ghost. Sometimes I get the impression that the world we live in, the world as depicted in novels and essays, seems to us purely and simply the kingdom of evil, as yet not divinized. Whereas a vision of genuine faith seems to me to demand that we view the world not only as wrestling with God but also as already making its way slowly toward Him, through the Incarnation. . . .

It's all too common to treat the priest as someone quite extraordinary, and the clergy itself, as well as the people, have got caught up in the game. . . . Few things anger me more than the claptrap that surrounds the priest's first Mass: Sacerdos in aeternum. It's not that that's extraordinary; it's the vocation of our mankind as a whole that's so extraordinary and wonderful. Forgive me if I quote in Latin a quotation from St. Bernard, difficult to put into French: Undique inhaerent Deus et homo, undique inhaerent perpetua et intima dilectione, tamquam inviscerati alterutrum sibi.* After that, who could dare set up a frontier of sacredness between two men? Especially as the one who is ordained needs so much to feel like a brother, and poor, and just one of them. . . .

* See note, p. 25.

Although Henri was entering fully into his retreat, he could not altogether absent himself from what was going on in the world and at 151. This letter is addressed to a friend of his seminary days who was editor of a local paper:

Ineuil, January 12, 1951

My dear Georges. I'm writing to you in view of the friendship which I think we both still feel. Some of the articles which you've already written, and of which my Mother sometimes sends me clippings, have surprised and astonished me.

I have on my table your article on the Warsaw Congress. I quite realize that you're making an effort to understand and not enter into open fight, and I admit that you've a right to reproach the Partisans of Peace with being, as you think, under the thumb of the Soviet Union. But I do not admit that you, a priest, have the right to print, in a paper that claims to be Christian, an article of the lowest type of journalism. You have no right to assume that the participants at the Congress were inspired by feelings of hatred; a number of my closest friends were there, people who are first-class Christians. Please have the courage to allow free correspondence in your paper, and let them give their own honest accounts. Then you can criticize them honestly in return. I am myself a member of the Partisans of Peace, and I know Y. Farge and other leaders. I myself took part in the Nice meeting, incognito, and I cannot admit that you're right to insinuate that these people are in bad faith. And you've no right to speak of the Abbé Boulier as you do; I was present with eighty priests and laymen at the church of Saint-Roch in Paris for his last Mass on September 9. You wouldn't write like this about him if you had been there too. A Christian's only right, as regards Abbé Boulier, is to adopt the attitude recommended by Mgr. Beaussard: to pray for him, to suffer with him in silence, and humbly to look for light—not judge him in the tone of proud and triumphant irony that you adopt. It is articles like yours that give Christians their tone of partisan complacency, which is such a betrayal of the Gospels.

Purely from a human point of view, if you are a regular reader of Bourdet's weekly, L'Observateur, you must be aware that these problems are far more complex than you let it be thought—in regard to the relations hardening every day between the United States and the Soviet Union, and (whether we like it or not) between capital and labor. May I refer you to the article on the Warsaw Congress in Number 34 of L'Observateur? It has the objectivity I would have liked to see in your article.

Please don't be offended by all this. I am saying it because we're friends. In communion with you in the Church of Christ.

Henri received the following reply:

January 19, 1951

My dear Henri. It was quite right of you to tell me frankly what you thought. It helps us to get reactions like yours now and again. Please don't think I feel the slightest ill will toward the Partisans of Peace. No doubt many of them are filled with sincere desire to spare the world another cataclysm. Here at Épinal we have a delegate from the Vosges who seems an excellent woman, and she speaks highly of the Warsaw Congress. But where I can't agree with her is when she accepts everything that comes from Moscow as being good.

Regarding Abbé Boulier, I only wish him well. But in the local Communist publications we are constantly being urged to follow him and admire what he writes. Now the fact that he is a pious priest in no way implies that he is right. What I regret is that he refuses to obey his Superiors. This attitude forbids us to follow him blindly.

We live in a time when the devil wears every possible disguise. I was wrong in my failure to moderate my words, and my main regret is that I've offended someone like you, whose only desire is to serve Christ in a genuinely Christian spirit.

When you are in these parts, do drop in and see me; we'll talk it all over, and you may do good to an old reactionary, which is what I remain in spite of all my good will to understand others and seek the truth on every side.

To Paul E.

Ineuil, January 27, 1951

Paul. Thank you for your wishes and your prayers. I spent Christmas among the three hundred inhabitants of a poor village in the Berry, and I had every reason to love the world. Like you, I live from one day to the next, without thinking about the future, consigning myself resolutely to Our Lord when I feel myself getting worried. My friends try to do the same, and we help each other. You must do so, too, and especially in what concerns Monette; I realize how hard the blow was and how it will make you suffer. Offer that, with everything else, to Our Lord, with the offering of each Mass. I shall do it with you, and it will turn to love.

Try to find the presence of Our Lord; everything is a sign of his presence for those who know how to love. But we love so little.

I don't yet know what will be the theme of our Youth Hostel study days, but the problem of all the suffering in which we live, of our attitude toward it, and what we can do about it, will surely be one of our governing ideas. As you know, it is my constant preoccupation.

I think it is one of the anguishes essential to the Christian —a gift of the Holy Ghost—this sense of the evil and sin that divide the world and make it suffer. It's already something to feel it, to be bowed down by it. It would be wrong always to bring the problem back to the question: What can we do about it? In many ways, we can't do anything; we won't conquer evil in this generation. But it's God who leads the struggle and those engaged in it; He gives us first and foremost a vision of his love and a certainty of it—even through our sin; a certainty that sustains us and will enable us often to find the action, the look, the support, the solution that others, without even knowing it, were expecting of us. The essential thing is an attitude of poverty, openness, unattachedness. . . .

To Paul E.

Ineuil, April 4, 1951

Paul. . . . Two points need further clarification, the question of unattachedness and the question of poverty. You link the two a little too much perhaps.

What does Our Lord expect of you? For the moment, it isn't at all clear, except that you must do everything possible to get better. As to the future, the point will be how to accomplish the gift of yourself that Our Lord is so clearly asking for. Through and with Monette, through and with another girl, or in some other way? The answer will come in its own time; try to free yourself from anxiety on the subject. I forget if you told me how you resolved the priest question —if it presented itself to you and how you resolved it. As for the marriage question, wait until you're better to solve it. And by the way I'd like to know where you stand, medically speaking.

The question of unattachedness, or being at God's disposal, is quite distinct from the question of poverty of spirit, although this brings with it a constant unattachedness. But I think you make a mistake when you think that evangelical poverty implies destitution, and yet more of a mistake when you think of giving up your job. If you should change your job, it should be for other reasons, which circumstances alone will show you. You mustn't accept destitution, either for yourself or for those dependent on you. On the contrary, you should seek to liberate from destitution everything that a true spirit of poverty enables you to acquire, and put money, goods, talents, friendships at God's disposal. We'll talk about this again, if you like, but it seems quite clear to me. . . .

In the spring, two events in the outside world were deeply upsetting to Henri. On April 7, 1951, a priest-worker, Michel Favreau, a docker at the port of Bordeaux, was killed by some timber being raised by a crane. Strong but hidden influences came into play to hush up the question of responsibility and to prevent blame being put on the port management.

The other event is reflected in the following letter:

To André F.

June 20, 1951

. . . As you say, the coming months are wrapped in obscurity. The way is not yet plain. But it will be in its good time: Our Lord will light the lamp.

In your silence, pray especially for Father F., who left the Church three months ago after a long and painful search. Ask those who bring up the subject not to judge him, but to love him still more, in prayer.

To Paul E.

Ineuil, June 23, 1951

Paul. I haven't hurried to answer your letter of May 22 because I thought that for the moment you must be so overwhelmed by Monette's acceptance. Deo gratias. I love your expression: "I feel empty, and very small." Yes, love comes suddenly, like a great torrent, and we feel all unprepared, like someone who's got a little bucket ready to receive it. I feel so happy for you, and for her. I hope the news will bring you joy and peace, and that it will give meaning and light to what you have been told about still two more years of rest, hence apparent inactivity. I hope also that it will strike new wells of hope and friendship in you, of openhearted welcome for others, and prayer with Christ.

I hope this joy doesn't intoxicate you nor unsettle you, but on the contrary will help you to pursue your reading and personal work, as well as your studies with the team you've formed. About the team, I really haven't much to say. What you do depends on the needs of each one of you, and these I don't know. I think it would be useful if you passed around Témoignage Chrétien, and discussed it. As for politics, I imagine you read L'Observateur and Quinzaine. I have just

finished Father Congar's book on true and false reform in
the Church. Some of the chapters might be useful to you.

For you personally, the spirituality of waiting, of engage-
ment. One day you must read *The Song of Songs*, which is
the song of married love, which will be yours, but through
which you will also hear the mighty voice of the love of the
Father for mankind.

I think that's all for today. Oh, yes, and this: think a great
deal about André E. and his wife, who are really going
through it at the moment, carrying their large part of Our
Lord's sacrifice. Go with God. I embrace you with a full
heart.

The following letter is to two young Youth Hostelers.
With Henri's help they had drawn close to each other and to
God. A few months later the man made his first Commun-
ion and the girl was baptized at 48 avenue de l'Italie.

Ineuil, June 11, 1951

G. Thank you for your letter of May 30, just before your
baptism. I can't tell you how happy I am, too, at having
been the person who helped you discover Christ and the
Church, and "revealed" to you the love of a God-Father
who loves men and shows us, in others, a reflection and sign
of his presence and love. These don't show themselves by
any sort of fanaticism or party spirit and still less by the as-
surance of ritual and mechanical salvation, but by a spirit
of faith, all inflamed with love and humility, which has infinite riches of strength and peace and openheartedness and
understanding.

. . . I insist only that you should be aware, especially as
Christians, that the riches that will be showered on you, and

that you will create, must overflow, and overflow onto all your friends and onto every hand that is stretched out toward you. You know that that's my hobbyhorse; and yet there's really nothing else important to say. It's nothing but the reiteration of St. John's "God is love." It's with that in view that my prayers envelop you and go with you during these weeks. When is the exact date of your marriage? June 23, I think. My heart will be there among you all . . .

VII

Leaving the Jesuits
July – December, 1951

It CANNOT be said that Henri Perrin was fully satisfied with his tertianship and retreat. Quite apart from his personal problem, he and a few of his colleagues failed to get the answer they were hoping for. They had lived their youth in the war, and the first years of their priesthood in conditions in which everything seemed to be called into question. Henri Perrin gained a great deal, as is evident from his letters, during his months of silence, prayer, and study. He was also able to make contact again with colleagues—also doing their tertianship—who were as enthusiastic as he about the working-class mission. When he left the Jesuits, as he now, slowly, did, his fellow feeling with them was in no way diminished.

What worried him and his friends was the inadequate adaptation of official doctrine and spirituality to the enormous needs that they had discovered, and to the immensely varied problems that disturbed them. They had come

153

across one or two outstanding masters of the spiritual life at the time of their novitiate and early studies. But teachers of such caliber are few and far between, and these young Jesuits found themselves left somewhat to their own devices and uneasiness during their tertianship. They could not see themselves following the pattern of teaching in a Jesuit school, or of preaching in the "classical" manner. The great human currents, they felt, did not pass that way. In their spiritual solitude they began to feel tempted to independence.

When his tertianship was over, Henri visited friends and relations, including his Carmelite cousin. The first thing that happened on his return to Paris was the death of Cécile.

Cécile Fournier, after trying to be a nun, joined up with Henri in *arrondissement* XIII in 1948, and worked there with passionate devotion. Shortly before Henri's departure for Ineuil she became utterly exhausted, and after endless examinations it was discovered that she had cancer. The specialist said she would die within weeks; in fact, she lived for a year.

Henri sent one of his group letters to announce her death.

Paris, September 17, 1951

Brothers. Perhaps you already know that Cécile left us last Thursday. I am sorry not to have let you know sooner. As Madame Fournier wanted the funeral to be a very quiet one, we couldn't send out the printed announcements earlier.

Because Cécile was so closely and deeply involved in our missionary work, I want to give you a few details about her last days among us.

You all know that Cécile had been confined to her bed

since September, 1950, condemned by the doctors, who diagnosed generalized cancer, to only another six weeks of life. However, she held on for a year—since January, with paralysis in her lower limbs. At the end of August, Father R. summoned me to Paris saying that Cécile's condition had worsened and that she might leave us any day. On September 2, she received extreme unction and offered her life for us all in the last Mass I celebrated in her room. The week of September 2–9 was passed in painful combat with the disease that had attacked her heart and head, and against the dullness of consciousness brought about by morphine injections. On the evening of Tuesday, September 11, she arrived fully conscious at the gates of death ("It's too terrible to die stifled; my God, give me a little more time") and peacefully offered her life "for XIII, for all the others, for the whole world; it's all one can do . . . My God, take me into your love." Our Lord let her glimpse the light ("Oh! what radiance, what light. . . . Why was I frightened of death?"). An injection kept her heart going and enabled her to survive the crisis. Wednesday passed in sleep, under the influence of morphine; on Thursday morning, without having to endure another access of pain, her heart gently stopped beating.

Cécile is the first of us to go back to the Father, bearing our sacrifice and our love. "Pray, brothers, that her sacrifice, which is also ours, may be acceptable to God, our Almighty Father." Far from laying us low, may her death be a source of confidence and help us to take the commitment of each day with yet more fidelity.

Let us all remain in brotherly union with each other and her.

To his Carmelite cousin

Vanves, September 19, 1951

My dear big Sister. You must have been anxiously awaiting a letter. First of all, thank you very much for my stay. I
enjoyed those calm days at your convent and was delighted
to be able to talk with you and the whole community. Keep
on praying for us. I am deeply convinced that our priest-
workers' mission is one of the most important events of our
time.

I enclose an account of Cécile's last days. She is now
watching over us.

I have had no difficulties with the Society. But I got back
to Paris at a very unfortunate moment, from the point of
view of finding a good landing-ground. I saw Monsignor
Feltin, who received me kindly but did not hold out much
hope, for various reasons that it would take too long to tell.
I told him that you were praying especially for him, and he
asked me to thank you. I continue to look for openings in
Paris, but at the same time I have got into contact with
Lyons and Marseilles.

Go on praying for me, but don't worry. Our Lord will
arrange everything as and when it pleases Him. Till we next
meet. I know that you won't write to me, but I shall write
to you. I remain your brother in Christ.

Vanves, October 15, 1951

My dear big Sister. Don't be cross with me for not having
written before. I hope you received the printed announce-
ment of Cécile's death. I put in a few words of my own—I
hope you didn't have to pay extra postage. In your silence,
I can feel your presence and your communion with me and

I thank you. The point of this letter is simply to give you a little news on your feast day.

In the six weeks since I saw you, Christ has been drawing me to Him with links whose solidity has constantly been tested. Far from upsetting me, the uncertainty of my future, together with various difficulties that are sometimes tragic, and difficulties no less tragic in which those around me find themselves—what struggles they often have—all this renews in me a great trust in Our Lord. I feel a great inner calm both toward the past and the future. In manu Dei.

My efforts to get accepted as a priest-worker in Paris or Lyons are continuing slowly. In Paris I must overcome a lot of obstacles which aren't personal to me but derive from the complex and delicate situation. If Christ wants me to be in Paris, He will fix things; if not, He will give me a clear sign in due course about where He wants me to be. In any case, although I have not officially left the Society yet, I feel it is an accomplished fact and I have no regrets. I am still living at the Action Populaire, and am not at all bored by this waiting, for greeting everyone again keeps me fully occupied.

I am reading Au Coeur des Masses by Father Voillaume of the Little Brothers of Père de Foucauld. I shall be sending it to you in due course. I think you will find in it some echoes of what I was trying to say to you.

And more than ever before, I entrust the mission of the priest-workers to your Carmelite prayers. . . .

A few words are needed here about the circumstances in which Henri Perrin left the Jesuit Order. The problem had already arisen when he left *arrondissement* XIII for his tertianship, and it became apparent that his Superiors had views different from his own (or at least hesitations) regarding the future of the mission he had undertaken, his personal vocation, and his return to the district.

Naturally, the involvement of some Jesuits—and other priests and religious, too—in the mission to the workers had not been carried through without difficulties, and this in spite of Cardinal Suhard's backing and prestige. Religious Superiors saw these activities as being for a time only, in each case, whereas the priest-workers themselves, because of the strength of their vocation and the demands made by working-class life, saw the activities as a commitment for life. Hence misunderstandings arose.

Moreover, it has to be admitted that Henri Perrin's temperament and the style in which he did things caused uneasiness. He was always ready to take bold initiatives. He faced material difficulties—such as getting 151 boulevard de la Gare going—with a sort of bland ingenuousness, trusting in his lucky star, in the devotion of his friends, and in his own undeniable "cunning." He *appeared* more incautious than he really was, more independent that he really felt; he *appeared* "anarchistic" and excitable, rather than calm and methodical—and yet . . .

Other attitudes he adopted, such as that during the strike of March, 1950, caused surprise. One of his Superiors wrote to him at the time: "The strike drags on with all its hardships, and I think you won't hold it against me if I feel a little uneasy about it. More than ever at this moment it behooves priest-workers to refrain from acting as if they were lay worker militants. Stay among the workers, of course, and in communion with them, but as a priest, without trying to make up for the militants' insufficiencies, without taking any purely temporal responsibility (unions, etc.)."

We may suppose that Henri Perrin explained himself and showed (as he did in his letter to Jean Cayeux quoted earlier) why and how the priest was obliged to state the claims of justice clearly. For a few days later this same Superior wrote to him: "I won't wait till tomorrow to thank you for your letter. I was rather dreading it. But your religious feeling has given it the impress of full and reciprocal trust. God will bless your humility and desire to be obedient, and you may rest assured that your workmates, to whom you have dedicated yourself, will benefit by your generosity. As for myself, I feel a bit like a staff officer telling a rank-and-filer how he should button his tunic!"

This example shows how Henri Perrin's dynamism could arouse concern and misunderstanding, and at the same time how his honesty and evangelical spirit could clarify the situation immediately.

In fact, his relations as a religious with his Superiors were normal. It was because of this, for instance—and because the mission in *arrondissement* XIII was so obviously important—that he obtained permission to postpone his tertianship from 1949 to 1950. It was on quite a different plane that the crisis in his year of retreat arose. Some light is cast on the situation by a letter from one of his Jesuit Superiors in December, 1950:

Henri. I am putting in writing what I said to you last night, in case you ever want to recall exactly what we said.

When I read the entry in your spiritual diary which you wrote after Father Provincial had told you that you shouldn't leave the Society, it seemed to me obvious that the attitude

of mind revealed by your words was not the one that the
Society expects of its members. Your way of stating the problem—as a choice between the Society and the Mission—
your way of arguing about it, and your deep emotional reactions are not those of a Jesuit.

That's why I said that if Christ didn't give you some
other illumination and attach you to the Society in some
other way, you had better ask to leave. For this would show
that you were not made for the Society.

It seems to me that to profit by your tertianship you must
pray that you may see whether your current attitude toward
the Society is really one of the highest generosity. If the
answer is No, then Our Lord will give you another light on
the Society and other links with it. If the answer is Yes,
which I personally am inclined to think after our conversation yesterday, you must ask to be released.

In order to examine this question, I don't think you need
wait to know Father Provincial's intentions as to whether
you will stay in, or leave, the workers' Mission. My fear
would be, if you did this, that you would be making everything depend on a decision exterior to the problem. The
really determining factor is your inner attitude, and this
is what you need to examine before Our Lord.

I told you yesterday how much I had prayed for you and
will continue to do so.

Your friend and brother, C.

Everything goes to show that the decision being made
during the summer of 1951 was a very painful one. We find
this in the letters he received from his closest friends, especially priests—both Jesuit and secular—who had been
closely associated in his best years in the Mission, and also

in his own notes. A parish priest to whose advice Henri attached the highest value wrote:

> August 7, 1951
>
> ... In my poor judgment you have been doing advanced reconnaissance work in this Mission which was both necessary and profitable, despite all the pitfalls and criticisms involved. But it seems to me that you owed your achievement, and the best of it, partly to the fact that you kept a firm link with the Church by means of the Society. This link is quite essential.
>
> Obedience is a rock, a guarantee, and a strength from God. . . . Dear friend, although I risk repeating myself, I would like to tell you again what the good Cardinal told me and impressed on me at Lourdes one evening in 1947: "The workers' mission must come about, for I can see no other way by which the mass of the workers can return to Christianity." If this or that sacrifice has to be made, and one which hurts badly, Christ may well expect it from a reconnaissance "scout" who is an example to other priests consecrating themselves to life in the workers' mission. . . .

A colleague in the novitiate wrote to him:

> August 21, 1951
>
> ... I can well understand the "heartache" you feel when you look into the future. As you say, the spirituality which will help you to win through, lies in conforming to the will of Christ; it is the spirituality of abandonment to God's will, of what St. Ignatius calls indifference: "I am still ready, O Lord, to remain in the Society if I knew that in this way I could give you greater glory." Or, better still, the spirituality

of the third degree of humility: "With you, Jesus, where You have shown that You were most alone, most forgotten, most misunderstood, most humiliated." In addition, there is the Blessed Virgin, to whom you have already often entrusted yourself. She will help you if we pray to her together.

Another advised him to wait:

October 3, 1951

... I was so distressed to hear about your difficulties. You know the friendship and esteem I feel for you.

The circumstances being as they are, with threats looming over the situation and so much prudence required, I don't think you should get yourself fixed up anywhere as a priest-worker. Couldn't you reach an understanding with your Provincial to give retreats for a year, or spend a year studying at Vanves? And meanwhile you could work out together how to reconcile your vocation to the Society and your desire to serve the workers. I don't think that leaving the Society at the present moment would do a service to the working classes.

Henri Perrin himself wrote:

... What I regret is that the one or two thousand souls in Paris, believers and especially unbelievers, who have attached themselves to me and who, through me, are slowly rediscovering the Church, these souls don't seem to be taken into account for a single instant. ...

As I see it, my request [to be a priest-worker] is a recognition of a situation that already exists: the fact that I have been working in Paris for three years and that I am bound

up with Paris and with work in the field of the Paris Church.
And the fact that I started being a priest-worker in 1943.

And so it was in order to maintain and develop all that
he had started in *arrondissement* XIII that Henri Perrin decided, after months of soul searching, to ask permission to
leave the Jesuits and become a secular priest again. Here is
another letter from a brother in the novitiate:

> October 20, 1951
> . . . I will never doubt the seriousness and depth of your
> decision. I will never view it as hotheaded or escapist. Our
> conversations have been enough to show me that you treated
> the matter on the only real plane possible. Do you remember
> some of our discussions on the mystique of obedience? For
> me they count among the really beneficial memories of our
> tertianship, which also, alas, has other memories. The atmos-
> phere was not ideal for anyone who wanted to grow in the
> full light of God. I feel partly responsible and would like
> to say how sorry I am.
> But while I have full confidence in your decision, I would
> like to say, because I want to be really frank, that I regret
> it for your sake. Not, I repeat, because I view it as a lesser
> spiritual good, nor because my faith in the Church is con-
> fined to an exclusive and complacent trust in the Society,
> nor because I have fixed ideas about vocations. My regret
> is that I think you have chosen an inconvenient way. You
> tell me that the steps you are now taking are complicated
> and long. I can well believe it—and more so than you say.
> If you'd stayed in the active Society (which you have not
> left, because you never really belonged to it), you might
> have found a quicker way out in spite of all appearances. But

.hat would have involved your passing, for a few years, through the test of the mystique of obedience, about which you once talked to me. Please understand that I'm not talking here of fidelity to grace, but of what is humanly practical as a way. Of the two alternatives I fear you have taken the most difficult one. And for this reason I shall always long to hear your news, and I hope we shall meet soon, because I remain your brother without any reserve.

Another of his closest companions wrote at the time of Henri's death, looking back to this period:

. . . We used to talk together a lot at the period when he was leaving the Society. Our conversations certainly in no way diminished the affection I felt for him. They enabled me to find out, or better, to understand more fully, his feeling of attachment to the world of the working classes and the deep charity that was its inspiration.

If our ways parted after that, it wasn't because he had lost merit in any way, nor because of the Society's lack of interest in the world of the working classes, but solely because his exclusive vocation to the world of the working classes ceased to coincide with the total "disposability" that the Society demands. When his vocation became something other than that of a Jesuit, it didn't cut him off from the many friends he had in the Society.

His Provincial wrote to Monsignor Feltin, Archbishop of Paris, in an effort to help Henri:

September 7, 1951
. . . For three years Henri Perrin was a priest-worker in

Paris in the area of the parish of Notre Dame de la Gare, and only ceased his activities to make his usual year of probation and tertianship.

In the course of his apostolate, Father Perrin's attachment to the Mission to the Workers developed and became deeper, so much so that it scarcely seems possible to reconcile it [any longer] with the entire "disposability" that the Society demands. But although he did not enter wholeheartedly into the spirit of the Society, this in no way diminishes the very deep qualities which can make him a very efficient apostle. He would like to be able to carry on his apostolate among the workers as a member of the diocesan clergy and especially those of the Paris Mission. He will shortly be calling on you about this.

After leaving the Society, Henri Perrin stayed on at Vanves and became more and more actively engaged in finding a bishop who would accept him as a secular priest. Both the Archbishop and the Provincial seem to have agreed that he should not stay on in Paris. A principle debarring former members of religious orders from Paris appears to have come into play. But, in addition, there was the extremely complex situation that had arisen in Paris and its suburbs, where there was a tendency for priest-workers (or those who thought they had this vocation) to proliferate. They included secular priests, regular priests, and, above all, priests who were more or less in an irregular situation. Six months earlier, on June 20, 1951, the Holy See had forbidden any increase in the number of priest-workers and had asked for an annual report on each of them personally from the bishop of the diocese in which they were working. The Paris Mission was quite ready to accept Henri Perrin and urged his case. But the Archbishop thought that the three or four Jesuits and Dominicans who were already priest-workers in *arrondissement* XIII, and had the support of two missionary parishes, could continue the work without Henri Perrin.

Meanwhile his former Superior in the Society was urging him to give up Paris and do everything he could to find some appointment in the provinces. He suggested Lyons as one of the most favorable archdioceses. He made the following points in a letter:

1. There are now various disadvantages to prolonging your stay in Paris: it sets too many people talking, and you have no effective authority.

2. It would be undesirable to press the Archbishop of Paris to go back on his decision. You are from the Vosges, but he is from the Franche Comté [both these parts of France reputedly produce stubborn temperaments].

3. Why cling to Paris, when your well-being seems to need something quite different? So far I have given you hardly any advice as to what you should do on leaving the Society, out of respect for your freedom. But as you are ready to listen to advice that urges you to stay in Paris, I feel at liberty to tell you straight that these advisers of yours (whom I don't know because you don't give me their names) can see no further than the ends of their noses. If they were more perceptive, they would, on the contrary, dissuade you from taking such a risk.

The risk, as I see it, is as follows:

You have exceptional apostolic qualities, a remarkable capacity for action, and an ardent and tenacious zeal. But this restless energy of yours needs to be canalized, moderated, given a direction.

Now in Paris the only real authority over you will be that of the Archbishop, and that will be too remote to play this necessary part in your activity. You see, the team is not enough; the team isn't the Church.

Henri Perrin decided to get in touch with teams in Marseilles and Lyons. He wrote to his friends:

Dear Friends. Following our conversation of yesterday, I am going to set down in writing some essential points of information on my present situation.

You know that after I had started my apprenticeship in Lyons in 1943, and after Germany, I was, from 1947 on, a priest-worker in Paris in the Jesuit team of Notre Dame de la Gare. I interrupted my work from September, 1950, until July, 1951, to do my tertianship. During this period, in full agreement with my Superiors, I asked permission to leave the Society. I would like to say two things about my leaving. It was due first and foremost to what I might call "incompatibility of temperament," that is, to the fact that I have a temperament unsuited to the religious life of the Society; second, and more important, to what my Provincial expressed in this way to Monsignor Feltin: "In the course of his apostolate, Father Perrin's attachment to the Mission to the Workers developed and became deeper, so much so that it scarcely seems possible to reconcile it [any longer] with the entire 'disposability' that the Society demands."

So you can see clearly the choice I made when I left the Society, a choice resulting from deep thought, much discussion, and constant prayer in the course of the year. It led me to ask to join the Paris Mission. Between 1945 and 1950 I had come more and more to agree with the ideas the Paris team was developing, and also with the way it did things. But in Paris I find myself up against three difficulties, and these are leading me to try to take up work elsewhere:

1. For internal as well as external reasons, the Paris Mission is unable to take me on at the present moment.

2. The Archbishopric, overwhelmed with requests from priests who have broken off from their own dioceses and Orders, is at the moment adopting a strict and negative policy.

3. I couldn't stay in Paris without creating an awkward situation between the Society and myself which my Superiors want to avoid.

For these reasons I am getting in touch with other French teams, notably those of Lyons and Marseilles, to ask them to explore the ground with their bishops to see if there is any possibility of my finding a landing-ground with them.

I don't think the directives of the Holy Office should prevent my doing this, as I have been employed in the workers' Mission since 1943, and the fact that my Diary of a Priest-Worker has recently appeared in an Italian translation will make those in Italy realize that I have belonged to the Mission for a long time.

This is what I wanted to explain. I thank you for your friendship from the bottom of my heart and entrust myself to your prayers.

After long delays Henri Perrin was able to meet Monsignor Lamy, Archbishop of Sens. At the request of Monsignor Feltin, he accepted Henri Perrin in his diocese. He recognized his vocation as a priest-worker and agreed that he should be allowed to join a worksite in the mountains for a few years. It was Henri himself who had heard about this work. It was at Notre-Dame-de-Briançon (Savoy), and the project was the building of the Isère-Arc dam. Hundreds of workmen were already engaged on it.

Henri was a man who acted promptly. In a few days he was ready to leave, and he said goodbye to Paris without fruitless regrets. He asked many of his friends to cease the correspondence they had developed with him while he was at Ineuil, in the hope that they would all soon be working together again in Paris. He promised to maintain the links by collective letters from time to time (a promise he kept until March, 1954). He stopped keeping the letters he received, as he had until now. He cut himself off, in this worksite which reminded him a little of Germany eight years before. "A camp, barracks, men of all races, especially North Africans and Italians, uprooted and without family, the brutalizing hours of work. I shall live there, silently, as long as Our Lord wants me to. I shall be there for Christmas. I shall think of all of you, whose prayers and friendship have followed me, step by step, for so many years. My prayers and friendship are yours always."

VIII

Priest-Worker at the Isère-Arc Dam (1952)

ISÈRE-ARC. These two words were destined to become famous, not only because of the immense dam completed in 1953 after about six years' work, but also because of the strike that broke out on the worksite soon after Henri's arrival at the end of 1951. There had been previous strikes, but the one that broke out in early 1952 was by far the most important and has a place in the history of the working-class movement in France.

Some account of the tremendous work involved in building this famous dam is required in order that Henri Perrin can be seen in the context of his next two years—years which constituted the culmination of his active life.

The daily paper, *Le Monde*, described the work as follows, in its issue of February 13, 1952.

The construction of the Isère-Arc tunnel and the generating station at Radens is one of the main aspects of the work centered around the upper course of the river Isère, and it will benefit by the regularization brought by the Tignes reservoir and, later, by that of the Champigny reservoir.

The dam, situated at the egress of the Pont-Seran gorges, creates a little lake some 70 feet deep. The pipeline, terminating at the gorge, begins by following the banks of the Isère as far as Notre-Dame-de-Briançon, flanking the slope first, then underground over a total length of nearly ten miles. The pipeline is of reinforced concrete 20 feet in diameter. The powerhouse, which is entirely underground, is composed of two stations. Each is supplied by a vertical steel-lined pipe 10 feet in diameter, and comprises two groups of generators supplying one group consisting of three monophase transformers. The annual production of electricity will amount to 450 million kilowatt hours. The work is expected to be completed by the end of 1953.

Further information on the work is provided in the preface written by Henri Perrin for the book of photographs published by the C.G.T. (the largest French trades union organization, Communist-dominated) at the time of the completion of the work.

As this book is written for the men who carried out this work, I will first describe the general characteristics of the achievement and then draw attention to the "human" aspect. For a dam and a tunnel are not only technical achievements; they are first and foremost a creation of men, a crystallization of the thought, the will, and the effort of thousands of men....

The technical aspect of the photographs must not lead us to forget the work of some 3,000 men—including managers, engineers, miners, and laborers—who enabled this enrichment of our national heritage to come into being. The work was often carried out in exceptionally difficult conditions because of the water and the heat, as well as the inadequacy of the pay at first—only slowly and painfully did wages reach a standard suited to the difficult and dangerous construction involved. The miners had to contend with mountain conditions and all the risks that they entail. And the work underground, which continued night and day, was of a nature to undermine the health of the hardiest. The "dam-boys" were also up against the nomadic life of huts and canteens, which gradually wear a man out as surely as factory life....

The photographs in this book are more than landmarks in a great technical achievement. They are reminders of many human things we do not want to forget. Alas, they are also reminders of the accidents that were the price of our achievement, and they commemorate the thirteen men who paid for the tunnel with their lives:

> Bortolo Carlassar, died November 10, 1948
> Smeca Angelo, died July 1, 1950
> Girard Louis, died June 8, 1951
> Madani Larbi, died October 30, 1951
> Medkour Amar, died November 14, 1951
> Bonnefoy Joseph, died January 4, 1952
> Ribeyre Camille, died March 3, 1952
> Bouaissa Mohamed, died March 29, 1952
> Cherouat Tahar, died July 20, 1952
> Bouceta Moussa, died August 14, 1952

Grim Mohamed, died January 4, 1953
Kadjetit Mohamed, died January 6, 1953
Juglair Attilio, died May 27, 1953

The following, from the Journal of the C.G.T., January,
1954, is a rough account of the disputes between the management and the workers up to the time of the 42-day strike
at the beginning of 1952:

In 1947 pay was poor, 55 francs an hour, with no extras.
Numbers of the workers soon began to agitate, and this led
to the foundation of a union group which included Balmain,
Allemand, and Franchino. They claimed a 4½ per cent
bonus because of geographical situation. In 1948 and 1949,
as the work got under way, the workers' "township" was set
up—canteens, workshops, dormitories—and the work on
the tunnel started. It was work for coolies; the men were
waist deep in water, their tools were of the roughest, and
there were no bonuses to speak of. An agitation was led by
Balmain, Allemand, Enrico, Hugues-Perrin, the Bals—
father and son—the inseparable friends Cotte and Ruffier,
Delpech (union treasurer), and others. The struggle began
for a water bonus. Arguments began with the management
and by August, 1949, a strike had broken out, voted unanimously, with pickets out. Better conditions of work were
obtained, but the movement only achieved its aims with
"the agreement of November, 1949," fixing working conditions in general.

The year 1950 passed calmly. The bonuses began to be
worth while. Wages averaged between 12- and 15,000 francs
per fortnight. In 1951, there started an endless story of
"sabotage," and the police were brought in by the manage-

ment to question the union leaders, which in no way diminished the combativeness of the latter. If things were patched up, discontent increased again toward the end of the year, when a bad patch of ground was encountered in the tunnel excavation, work was slow, and bonuses fell down to nothing. At the beginning of 1952 a new strike started which lasted 42 days and ended in a victory for the unions.

A worker who went to Isère-Arc some months after Henri Perrin, wrote as follows:

The B. worksite at Notre-Dame-de-Briançon was, at the beginning of May, 1952, emerging from a long and severe strike which had lasted 42 days. My first impression was extremely unfavorable. Although I had had thirteen years' experience of public works in various parts of France, I had never before worked in conditions like these and had never come across a boss with so little respect for the workers and their organization. Never before had I seen union leaders so timid toward the management, nor men working like convicts at the cost of life and health in an atmosphere of humidity, extreme changes in temperature, gas, dust, and mud, to the infernal noise of the pneumatic drills and cement mixers. Never before had I had the experience of leaving work wet through, in winter, and finding nothing in the huts to dry the clothes you had to put on again next morning. I'd never found it so difficult to sleep as in those dormitories. And the men who'd been there for several years said: "If you'd been here before our strike you would have found it much worse." Sometimes it is hard to believe that in a country like ours there are still bosses like B. to whom the machinery is more important than the men.

A collective letter from Henri Perrin to his friends

Christmas, 1951

. . . So I left Paris on Friday evening after a goodbye to
the Society, which, I would like to repeat, was enormously
brotherly. I left Paris and XIII against my will, certain that
there was a mistake, even if a providential one. The following morning I arrived at Notre-Dame-de-Briançon and went
straight from the train to sign on. At 1:30 in the afternoon,
I began work as a mechanic, mending pneumatic drills at
the entrance of the tunnel.

The Isère-Arc tunnel was begun in 1947. It is 10 miles
long and will take at least another year to be completed. The
firm of Borie employs over 400 men at each end of the
tunnel. Of all nationalities, they are accommodated in the
sort of barracks I know well. Work goes on night and day,
including Sundays. I worked last Sunday for the first and last
time. My minimum is a 51-hour week for a basic wage of
115 to 125 francs an hour.

I've been in touch with the village priest, who welcomed
me warmly. He fully understands my position and his house
is always open to me. In view of the circumstances here, he
fully agrees that I should remain incognito for some time,
and my experience of the first few days makes me think this
will be possible. There is another Henri Perrin on the worksite, a foreman. Letters are distributed in bulk at the canteen;
mine would pass through fifty hands before reaching me. So
I would like to be written c/o Madame B. or Mademoiselle
W., who will keep my letters for me.

I've been put in a dormitory with four people. It is over-
heated and entirely decorated with Paris-Hollywood nudes.
There is a good old Spanish grandfather, a half-caste, and

two young fellows from Romans. Yesterday, Christmas
night, I strummed a bit on my guitar; we ate your chocolates,
drank the local priest's bottle, and then went to sleep. I've
slept a lot in the last three days because when I arrived here
I was completely done in. There are a lot of North Africans
here. I'm glad that I have plenty of time and can make my
contacts slowly and naturally.

During these last days I've kept feeling that I must be
mad to be doing this. It's true. Before I left, one of my
friends told me that at times I hadn't got both my feet on the
ground; but, hang it all, who would say that the Church has
both feet on the ground when she asks us to do it! This
cheers me up, and in the last three days I've not felt depressed at all—any more than I've felt any great enthusiasm.
I live as best I can, and that's already something. . . . God
bless you all at the end of the year.

January 3, 1952

. . . I am slowly finding my feet in this forgotten corner of
the world. I've had reassuring letters from my former Superiors, as well as from the present ones, the Bishops of Sens
and Moutiers. And these make me feel confident. Last Sunday I met the three priest-workers from Tignes at the Dominican house in Chambéry. A really brotherly day talking
things over with the Prior. I hope soon to be able to go and
see the Bishop of Moutiers.

On the job I've been moved from mending pneumatic
drills to mending electric tractors. The work is entirely new
to me, and I have to learn it almost unaided. It's interesting,
and I shall learn a lot about machinery before I'm through.
My first fortnight will be up in four days' time, and I'll be
getting my first pay packet. I haven't found out much about

anyone yet. Like them, I don't talk much. You make friends slowly, in spite of the communal life. The day before yesterday an old Spaniard asked me if I'd ever been in prison. Someone had told him I'd just left prison after thirty years! Others had told him that I was a priest who had got a woman with child and run away.... We smiled.

This world of big public works is a world of its own. There are thousands of men in the region, and no one looks after them. They're not casual labor; this is where they live— until the next job. In the spring a lot of them will be going off up to Tignes, where the pay is better. But what a life!

In the evenings I go to the village priest's house. He lives with his sister and mother, and they have adopted me. He has given me his spare room and I say Mass there between 6 and 7 in the evening. Then we have a bit of a chat. All this is fine.

I think that I'll be spending the whole of 1952 here. I feel in fine form, both spiritually and physically. I can't imagine why, but I feel an astonishing peace, and really on the right path—I'm sure we're right. Without this conviction and joy, no one would be able to endure life here. God put me here. Pray for me as I'm praying for all of you at the outset of 1952.

To his Carmelite cousin

Notre-Dame-de-Briançon,
January 4, 1952

My dear big Sister. You must be wanting to have a letter from me in spite of the news Mother sends on to you. I had meant to write you before Christmas, but things happened too quickly.

The first thing I want to say is that I'm happy, and after

the three months I spent waiting about and looking around, I now have a clear path before me—with Christ, I feel sure. Things took such a long time only because I didn't want to leave Paris before I'd done everything I could to stay there, just as I'd made up my mind to do everything possible to remain a priest-worker before accepting a post in the parish clergy.

By and large I have no reason to complain of anyone. Everyone has been very decent to me, especially my Superiors, my former Paris parish priest, and the Bishops of Sens and Moutiers. It wasn't too much of an ordeal, and finally everyone was in agreement. My Superiors took the view that it had been a mistake for me to join the Jesuits, and the Society is as fond of me as ever. In a word, I am more than ever convinced of the truth of our priest-workers' vocations, and I beg you, as I did in September, to pray and make others pray for our intention. Taken as a whole, the Mission is in good shape.

I won't give you any more details about my life here because you'll be hearing them from Mother. But I'd like you to know that I feel very much at peace, and in the hands of Christ, among all these men of every race in this gigantic enterprise. When I got to the site this morning, I found a man had been killed—he was only twenty-two; he fell into the sand of the cement works and was suffocated. As you see, our world isn't always a quiet one.

What about you? I think of you, I count on you, and I'm waiting for your annual letter. Through you I would like to express my great confidence in you to the Mother Superior and the whole Carmelite convent, and I promise you my poor prayers. Go with God. May the Holy Ghost unite us. With enormous brotherly feeling.

In his solitude at the outset of his new life, Henri wrote
to his friends in Paris more often than he had foreseen:

January 10, 1952

*Some more news. What I'm writing to you is a kind of
diary. Thank all of you who sent me wishes, and everyone
who prays for me and for our cause. I'm writing to you in the
canteen, surrounded by 400 of the boys, who are having a
lively general meeting. The workers' representatives are dis-
cussing wage claims with the boss. This may result in at least
a token strike. So far it seems that the union activity has
been rather weak. But the day before yesterday the representatives woke up, and the mass of the men seems to be ahead of
them. I've never seen a meeting like this except during the
general strike. Of course the collective life of the "township"
makes things much easier here.*

*As for me, I get deeper every day into the life of this enter-
prise. During the past week I've felt rather like a bolt being
screwed a little further into a mass of metal each day. Faces
open out slowly, those of a sub-proletariat with a very special
kind of life: young people without any attachments, Italians,
Spaniards, and North Africans, and men of a certain age who
are either foremen or have been left behind by life.*

*Our life is hard, harder than people realize. The work it-
self is hard, and the communal life—all of us jammed together—is hard. One longs for a room of one's own, a thing
which seems a minimum requirement for living a man's life.
I haven't yet got a cupboard, and I'm not the only one. Besides, there are risks. Six men have been killed since the work
began. The most recent was the boy killed last week, buried
and suffocated in the sand of the cement mixer. We had a
half-day's slowdown in token of mourning.*

My work is becoming more and more exacting. There's no need of a foreman; the work itself takes command. The machine must be kept running, so must the tractors, and so Perrin and the others have to do their job. On Tuesday I had to work for 12 hours, on Wednesday 11, today 10, and we usually have to work on Sundays, too. Besides, you get caught up in the game. You are responsible for your job. If I failed, the brakes wouldn't work; if the electricians failed, the floodlight wouldn't work; and the life of our workmates depends at every moment on floodlights and brakes. Besides, I'm learning a whole mass of technical things. I'm always having to muddle my way through alone, and I'd be stuck ten times a day if my mates weren't there. Don't worry about the cold. In the last fortnight I haven't had time to feel cold. Besides, Notre-Dame-de-Briançon is only about 1,200 feet up.

For the rest, I do a bit of practice on my guitar every day—not enough. If I could play properly, this evening, while we're waiting for our union representatives, I'd have an enthusiastic audience of 400 of the boys. All around the mountain looms over us, calmer and more silent than ever; 3- or 4,000 feet of almost vertical rock, and behind it there's the snow. I went alone to say hello to it last Sunday.

Last week I spent an evening with the Bishop of Moutiers. He is friendly and understanding and prepared to listen to our problems. He read me Monsignor Ancel's plan for a directive for the priest-workers. He keeps his heart and his house wide open to us. It's all fine. In ten days' time I'm due to meet the other priest-workers again at Moutiers.

That's enough for today. May the Holy Ghost preserve all this business in our hearts and so enable us to take a part in the redemption of the world.

Notre-Dame-de-Briançon,
January 20, 1952

My dear Friends. I feel I must send you a fourth letter already. We are out on strike. I enclose the text of the appeal which will be forwarded to the press tomorrow and published as a leaflet.

You will think that I'm at the bottom of this! But you'll be wrong. The technical problems connected with bonuses are unknown to me, and until last Friday I didn't think any prolonged opposition would be possible. But now it's happened, and we're up to our necks in it.

After I had spoken two or three times on matters of procedure, I found myself elected to the committee, and for the last three days I've been acting as its typist. In addition, of course, I'm a member of the solidarity commission. I've managed to avoid joining in the discussions with the management for many reasons. What is so exciting, and so moving, is the sudden trust that has suddenly come into the eyes of my workmates. As for the committee, I take off my hat to it. It contains a dozen worthwhile militants, and their own conflicts and resentments have been melted by the strike like snow in summer. And there's no question of our being "led by the nose." The presence of our Spanish mate, Diaz, is by itself a guarantee that no one is carrying on a personal policy of any sort in the strike. It's a real strike that follows all the rules of art and of the moralists. Anyway, read our declaration, get others to read it, and try to talk about it in the press. I'll keep in touch with you about it. Pray for us as I do for you. With all my affection.

Here is the text to which Henri Perrin refers in the above letter:

Strike at the Isère-Arc tunnel

A strike has broken out at the B. worksite engaged in piercing the Isère-Arc tunnel at Notre-Dame-de-Briançon and Aiguebelle. In deepest winter, over 1,000 workmen have downed tools. No one can remain indifferent, and it is our duty to explain why over 1,000 workers are prepared to accept hardships and to fight to be treated like men.

First, a brief account of the facts. For months the workers have been trying to obtain a statute which recognizes the work involved in constructing the largest tunnel in Europe. During the last ten days the workers' representatives have been trying to reach a solution. On Wednesday the men walked out and, as the management refused to give way on essential points, felt obliged to stay out for 48 hours. On Friday an unrestricted strike was decided on at Notre-Dame-de-Briançon; and on Saturday, Aiguebelle followed suit.

Why is this? Because pay is too low, especially in view of the dangers involved. Because the conditions of work and accommodation, of hygiene and safety are inadequate and unfit for human beings. Because the management fails to fulfill its commitments, or hoodwinks its employees with promises that never materialize.

Low wages, which bonuses, doled out in driblets, do not augment sufficiently to compensate for the effort involved and the risks run.

Harshness of the work, day and night, in water, dust, gas, and heat. The worker on the sites leaves his hut at 5 A.M., to return to the canteen at 3 P.M.

Danger of the work, especially at four miles under the mountain. Five men have died as a result of accidents on the worksite in less than a year, not to mention all the lesser accidents.

Unhealthiness of the work and the accommodations, where we are five in the small rooms, and forty-six in the communal room, where the comings and goings of men on different shifts make sleep almost impossible.

Harshness of living conditions for all those men who, in order that they and theirs may live, find themselves far from their families, exiled and rootless in this corner of France, which should be so peaceful for man. Harshness of life, especially for our Spanish, Italian, and North African workmates: the worker is not even in his homeland; he has the guarantee that he can use his hands, but otherwise he has nothing but insecurity and loneliness. Who can deny our right to demand human conditions, and especially for the foreigners that France has taken in? Who can deny the right of men to be respected and not reduced to mercenaries or slaves?

As a result of these things, we are claiming a pay increase of 20 per cent, the signing of collective agreements to guarantee our work, and the application of a sliding rule to guarantee the stability of our wage in relation to the cost of living. We are claiming living conditions in which a human being can at least have some rest, since he cannot return to his family at night. We are claiming solid guarantees proportionate to the risks we run in serving the community.

As a result of these things and because we know that our struggle is everyone's struggle, we call on everyone for solidarity—on the civil, religious, and professional authorities of the population among which we are living. We appeal to everyone—agricultural workers, artisans, and tradesmen —to help us in our struggle. We appeal above all to our mates in factories and on worksites, and to our mates in the various union centers.

We thank them in advance, and hope that with their help our struggle may soon end, and that the men may be able to live and believe in the brotherhood that unites all men.

                                                        The Strike Committee

P.S. All gifts, whether in money or kind, should be addressed to the Strike Committee, Township B., Notre-Dame-de-Briançon, Savoy, or else be handed to collectors who will call, or to union centers, municipal authorities, or parish priests.

As the strike continued, Henri Perrin rapidly became to all intents and purposes the committee secretary. It is largely to his pen that we owe the almost daily communiqués issued by the committee. Only a selection can be quoted, as all together they would make up a small volume.

Extract from Communiqué No. 1

. . . Our pay packets issued on Monday give us the opportunity to prepare ourselves calmly. We must first begin to organize solidarity among ourselves, and from Monday on, those in better positions must get ready to help the others. On Tuesday an appeal for solidarity will be promulgated by the press and communicated to people in a position to be of help to us. Individual workmates will be given the task of getting into touch with these people, and at the same time collection teams will be assembled. A printed leaflet will be handed out to you to be distributed as widely as possible. An account of all monies received and distributed will be kept scrupulously up to date, and any individual can ask to see it when he wishes.

The committee will sit in Savoldelli's room. All information and communication will be centralized there. There will always be a workmate at your disposal there.

We wish to draw attention to the fact that a number of workmates, above all the French, have not yet stopped work —mechanics, tractor drivers, and rail layers. Anyone who knows of such cases should make every effort to convince these men of their mistake. . . .

Extract from Communiqué No. 3

Our own collection will be made this afternoon from everyone employed here, whether on strike or not. This collection must amount to at least 300,000 francs.

Cases of urgent need should be submitted to the following workmates: for the North Africans, Taouche and Boubsah; for the Spaniards, Diaz; for the Italians, Mario Badoni; for the French, Bernard, Jourdain, or Perrin.

Collecting in the region will be undertaken when public opinion has been prepared for it through the press, visits to prominent people, and leaflets. This afternoon workmates will be chosen to contact personalities in the region, beginning tomorrow. Collecting will be carried out by teams equipped with receipt books from Thursday on.

Extract from Communiqué No. 4

Canteen. Midday meal. There will be two services, at midday and at 2 o'clock. Workmates are asked to divide themselves up between these two services.

Evening meal. In conformity with decisions already taken, this meal costs 50 francs. Special tickets are on sale at the counter. These tickets, or the price of the meal, will be collected by specially delegated workmates. We ask our workmates to abstain from ordering meat.

Our North African workmates have offered to contribute their wine at the midday meal for the benefit of the strike.

The Isère-Arc strike had wide repercussions beyond the locality, and was widely discussed in France. The regional newspapers printed in full, or gave résumés of, the strike communiqués. These were taken up by the national dailies, from the liberal *Le Monde* to the Catholic *La Croix;* and weeklies such as *Témoignage Chrétien* and *La Vie Catholique* printed long articles on the subject. On February 19, 1952, *La Croix* said: "When one reads of these living conditions, one is astonished that the revolt did not occur earlier." The Bishops of Annécy, Chambéry, and Moutiers issued their own special communiqués. The sympathetic response among the local population resulted in hundreds of workers, hitherto regarded as "foreigners," being absorbed friendlily into the life of the region. In this, as in many other events, we can see the influence of Henri Perrin and a few associates. From the first day of the strike, he himself began mobilizing friends near and far.

On January 28, the thirteenth day of the strike, the committee argued for ten hours with the management in the presence of officials from the Ministry of Works. But the management refused to give way on the principal claims of the workers.

Notes for a communiqué, found among Henri Perrin's papers

. . . *The regional press and the Paris press, union and workers' organizations, Catholic movements and Communist groups—all have expressed their solidarity with the*

1,000 workers on strike. Following the Bishop of Moutiers, the Archbishop of Chambéry expressed sympathy and support for the workers. The Ministry of Works has agreed to try to find grounds for settlement, and the workers' representatives spent the whole of Sunday in an attempt to persuade the management to listen to their point of view. The management had offered an increase of 80 francs a day for unskilled workers doing night shifts in the tunnel. In view of this lack of comprehension on the part of the management, the workers have drawn closer together and are entering the third week of the strike they did not want.

. . . They are being helped by men who understand their problems and difficulties. There is, for instance, a surgeon at Albertville who has offered to attend them for nothing and has contributed 2,000 francs. There is the manufacturer at Chambéry who has contributed 9,000 francs, and the baker at Briançon who delivers 100 kilos of free bread. They are also being helped by a Catholic organization of Chambéry which is forming a solidarity committee on the initiative of Abbé V., and by the Communists whose spirit of brotherhood is beyond description. . . .

Letter from Henri Perrin to the management of worksite B.

Sirs. At the conclusion of the fourth week of a dispute that you deplore as much as we do, and in view of the slow pace of negotiations which the strikers, more than anyone, have reason to wish rapidly concluded, I would like to make a summary of the past four weeks of the strike.

The Strike Committee wishes to lodge a bitter complaint regarding the slowness of negotiations. It is intolerable that the first commission of employers should have delayed ten days before hearing us, and the second commission twelve days—despite the extreme pressure brought by the workers' delegation. This happened at a time when 1,100 families were affected by the strike.

We fully recognize the points which have been gained in the course of the strike, but we think that many of these points should have been gained without any need for striking.

As regards the "township" in particular, no one denies the lack of amenities which has resulted in the present state of things. We have noted the promises made by the management, and you may be sure that we shall make it our business to see that they are carried out in the months to come. We have been offered a standard indemnity for our discomforts—600 francs. But we would like to point out that at an earlier stage the management charged 128 francs a day for the hire of a bed in our rooms.

As regards wages, you and managements of other worksites have stated on a number of occasions that you would support our demand for an increase and that you thought it justified. Hence we are astonished that through the press you could make propaganda about "average wages" (what are they?) and thus renew the myth about "high wages at the dams" in the eye of public opinion. This can only misrepresent the real meaning of our strike.

As regards the bonus for output, the workers are unable to forget that it has remained unchanged since 1949, except for an increase of 8 francs last year. Every day it becomes more deflated as compared with wages which, as you yourselves have admitted, have increased during the same period by 70 per cent. And, as you yourselves have admitted, wages are not yet in line with the increased cost of living.

. . . There are other points on which there is still deep disagreement—for example, the subject of the cement factory. Here the workers, despite a month's strike, have obtained virtually no visible increase, although they had no say in October on the matter of their average output. The workers would like to repeat that when they resort to exceptional means, such as a strike, they do so at the price of great sacrifices and with the determination to achieve such substantial changes as will allow them to live a decent life and one with some relationship to the risks they run. At the beginning of the strike you said you always wanted to do the maximum for the workers. In our opinion you now have an opportunity to do so.

Negotiations which took place from February 22 to 25 led to an agreement in principle which was signed on the morning of February 25. On February 26, the General Assembly of the strikers ratified the work of their representatives and were back on the job the following morning.

A communiqué, drafted by the Strike Committee and Henri Perrin, was sent to the press announcing the end of the dispute.

The Isère-Arc dispute has now ended after a 42-day strike. On the morning of February 25 a new agreement was signed at Aiguebelle. . . .

By signing this agreement the workers' representatives aimed at offering a proof of good sense and clear-sightedness. The day before, the workers had again voted in a secret ballot for an unlimited continuation of the strike for an 8 per cent special increase. But the Committee is convinced that on this point it would come up against a Government veto. It is aware that the continuation of the dispute by means of a local strike might result in defeat over wage claims and possibly even to the loss of the advantages already obtained. Under these circumstances it considers that it would be criminal to prolong the strike, and asks the workers to continue the struggle in the usual form of negotiations at the worksite.

. . . The strike has achieved three essential gains. Regarding the reorganization of the "township," the victory has been almost complete, with the construction of five new dormitories, of a drying room, of a recreation room, and an indemnity of 10,000 francs for hard living conditions; regarding displacement, a bonus has been obtained for major displacements in the cases where this applies; and regarding the output bonus, a 60 per cent increase has been obtained —with all bonuses indexed to wages. Various other increases have also been won.

. . . The Isère-Arc workers return to work with the consciousness of having forged their unity in battle, ready to continue the struggle side by side with their fellow workers. They have made their own small impression on the general struggle. . . .

Notre-Dame-de-Briançon,
March 6, 1952

Dear Friend. No sooner had I arrived here than I got down to work (in the first fortnight of January, I did 120 hours, that is an average of 10 hours a day including Sundays); then came the strike, to which the press devoted a good deal of space on a number of occasions, which by the force of things made me secretary, with all that that involves in work and responsibility. At the same time, through an indiscretion on the part of the police, it became known that I was a priest; and today, on the occasion of the funeral of the seventh of our workmates killed within a year on the site, I performed my first official religious act.

My God, what a life! I am committed to the worksite to the end; that is to say, the beginning of 1954. I have no regrets—far from it. I have solid support from the Bishop of Moutiers, the village priest, my workmates on the site, and the friendship and support of all those whom I have left behind me.

Notre-Dame-de-Briançon,
March 15, 1952

Dear Everyone. Here's another collective letter, which is a way of avoiding repeating the same things over and over again to individuals.

We are now fully out of the strike, and the results regarding my pay are gratifying. I earned 6,000 francs in the last three days; that is to say, for 30 hours' work. But above all, what we have gained is that the management has really got going, that the worksite is running better than ever before, that there are constant adjustments in the organization of the work, and that the "township" is growing under our eyes. Better still, the bosses, far from trying to make reprisals, treat the strike leaders with obvious respect. They consult us and listen to us. In a word, the situation is good. A new fatal accident that occurred four days after our return to work (one of us was crushed by a tractor in the tunnel) served to reinforce the attitude of the workers and the situation I have just described.

As far as I am concerned, all is well, and Christ seems to be taking a guiding hand in events. From our workmates I get an esteem and trust often amounting to friendship, which overwhelms me and makes me ashamed. The smile and the handshake of our workmates, whether those of the union, or the Spaniards or North Africans, is my best reward and consolation. It would be impossible for me to want to get away soon. The management, too, has started playing the same game. On a number of occasions the manager has come to have talks with me, has told me of his plans, and has asked me what the workers think of them.

The funeral of our workmate also marked a new stage for me. Inevitably, I had to officiate at it myself. All the workers were present, when I appeared all dressed up and ornamented, before a great number of workmates who were not yet aware that I was a priest. Half of them came into church; the other half stayed outside. When we emerged, some of them came up to me and said that in the view of all, or nearly all, the ceremony had increased the trust they felt in me. As in addition to this I've had an opportunity of spending a long evening with the Bishop of Moutiers, I am now in an exceptionally good situation. . . .

I am very tired, but slowly getting better (I'm taking a tonic), and work takes up a lot of time. But this is nothing compared with the expressions of friendship that my workmates are showing me and the possibility of work ahead of us in really good conditions.

I hope you will thank Our Lord, as I do. I shall be praying with you for you all and for all those who are dear to us. . . .

P.S. Here's the latest. On his way back from work the union secretary told me that the undermanager, who is always shouting at others, even by his own admission, told the workers' representatives not to be afraid to shout at the foremen who are not doing their work properly!

Good Friday, April 11, 1952

Dear Everyone. Never before have I had a Good Friday like this, with 11½ hours' work in the first heat of spring and all kinds of annoyances. I now understand for the first time the extent to which these men—working today as usual —must feel remote from the liturgy of this season as carried out in the churches. Even on Sunday a lot of them will be working.

. . . Thank you for all your letters. I'm sorry indeed to have to answer them all together. There are no meetings in the evenings, but after the day's work there are jobs to be done for the union. Last week we had our eighth death; one of our workmates was crushed by a rock in the tunnel. There was widespread feeling and solidarity for the four children left behind by this North African workmate.

. . . Luckily I'm feeling fine. In addition I have made closer and closer friendships and feel the growing sympathy of the North Africans. The atmosphere here is very different from that of the Government!

I am planning to spend Easter at Thonon with the B's. I'm delighted to hear that the Alpes-Berry camp will be held in the Tarentaise, and I'm looking forward to going to join it one Sunday in August. I've lent 40,000 francs to two workmates who were in a fix. If there's anyone who can pay me back, or from whom I've asked for money, I hope they won't forget me. I'd like to be able to buy the typewriter I used during the strike, and I shall need funds. . . .

May Our Lord bring us all increase in faith and charity. I embrace you all in the joy of Christ.

Notre-Dame-de-Briançon,
Ascension, May 22, 1952

Dear Everyone. Nothing much fresh has happened in the weeks since Good Friday, but I want to write to you, thinking of each of you personally as if we were having a quiet conversation alone together.

Materially, life goes on the same at Isère-Arc. I'm always in the workshop doing hack jobs, which makes life tiring at times. . . . I've managed to get union collectors and representatives appointed, and they're doing their work very well. Nearly all the boys in the workshop are in the union now. I've given my Bishop food for thought over the answer I got from my representative, a practicing Catholic, when I asked him to go and see the boys in his sector individually: "I agreed to be a representative, but don't count on me for rounding up the boys; if you want generous fellows who are concerned about other people, get them from the union; it's their job."

On the whole, the work is going well, the rock is of good quality, the tunnel is progressing, the bonuses are fairly high. But there are daily rows about all kinds of things—taking men on, dismissing them, claims, and so forth. The sixteen representatives are beginning to get the hang of things. Union life is getting organized with the nomination of the collectors, and the number of membership cards is already double that of last year.

. . . In view of the uneasiness that even the hierarchy feels about us, I would like to underline what I've experienced here regarding the educative value of work in a union. I see it as the direct and spontaneous expression of all that is best in the aims of the workers. Men who devote themselves to work in the unions almost inevitably become transformed by it; even their characters change.

For us priest-workers, playing our part in this work is not a mere helping out, and even less an opportunity for making contacts, but a real demand of an apostolic kind. If this could be acknowledged, there would be less hesitation and far more understanding of our mission.

At the moment we are very disturbed by Government policy. For the first time, perhaps, we here are feeling direct repercussions of the policy pursued in Paris: unemployment, which is going to become serious in the coming months (the dams alone are going to release some thousands of workers in the region); the freezing of wages, which might be revised in Savoy without formal orders from the Government to the prefects; the cessation of public works resulting from the fact that the national economy is bled white by war and rearmament; difficulties over foreigners' work permits, with the object of expelling them and thus camouflaging unemployment; the terrible problem of unemployed North Africans, who live clandestinely in the "township" and queue up every day to be taken on and every day are turned away. This is not a question of party politics; we are up against serious human problems with deep influence on the lives of individuals. What is a Christian to think about a world which has ceased even to guarantee the right to work? Moreover, all the echoes that reach us here from outside make us feel we are in full "reaction." How shall we get out of it?

Yet over and above the anguish of the general political situation and the demands made by life in the union, I am meeting men, with their difficulties and, as I discover every day, with their richness, their delicacy, their good will—and often crushed by a thousand circumstances for which God

alone knows how responsible they are. Some day I would
like to write a novel called The Children of God—of course
I never shall! But the further I go and the more contact I
make with men, the more sympathy I feel for them, and the
more I discover possibilities which to most people would
seem small indeed, but which are yet a manifestation of the
Father's love.

I would like to go on talking to you, but a North African
workmate whose wife is in the hospital has begun telling me
about his difficulties with a French family.

In a little while I shall be going to church to say the evening Mass for the parish. I shall be praying with you all. You
know what the Communion signifies, in these days when the
Church makes us praise the one who "set his people free."

To Paul E. and Monette
                                        August 6, 1952
    . . . So your marriage is drawing near. I am so happy, and
am praying for you, thinking of you preparing for it with
joy and in the slow communion of your two lives.

Don't worry about tomorrow. Just try to overcome the
difficulties of today. Try calmly and without losing heart to
get the upper hand over each day's difficulties, and the rest
will come like a gift from God.

I've been back on the worksite for a fortnight, in peace
and joy, and in the union activity which you are familiar
with and which I feel more and more to be an indispensable
part of the worker's life.

And you? What are your plans? Where are you living?
Are you surrounded by those necessary friends who make
the road so much easier and are one of the best signs of the
Father's presence?

However, you will be seeking before everything the communion of your two personalities, of your souls, your bodies, and your temperaments. It is a delicate task and you may be assured of my prayers and my deepest feelings.

Notre-Dame-de-Briançon,
August 18, 1952

Very dear Friends. An iron bar which fell on my leg has given me a fortnight's rest from work. I'm returning tomorrow. But I've had an excellent opportunity for sorting out all kinds of questions about the worksite, for following more closely the various discussions in progress with the management, and for making a leisurely trip to Paris to bless the marriage of C. and Jacqueline, and for practicing on my guitar a little.

On July 11, I was our union representative in Paris at the meeting of the Central Committee of the firm. I mention it for the record, for it was all a bad joke. The financial statement was dealt with in three minutes without anyone's raising a single query. On the rare occasions when the members of the Committee asked a question, the final answer always was, "Monsieur B. has decided that . . ." When I was bold enough to speak myself, I was reminded that I was only there for purposes of consultation!

On the worksite we are passing through a period of claims, above all for an improvement in the bonus for working in concrete and for piercing the upper part of the tunnel (to take place soon). We are still in the middle of negotiations, with a crucial meeting expected next Tuesday or Wednesday. As the weeks pass, the lack of initiative or training of both the workers' and the management's representatives is becoming more obvious; if they were more active, a lot of matters could be dealt with quickly. As things are, I have had to intervene in numbers of matters and spur on the management—and at times this works like a boomerang! Last week the boss thundered at me, and the next day we had a long discussion which was intended to be friendly (it took place in the presence of the representatives), about the questions under dispute.

This is holiday time and you can feel that the worksite is tired and things have slowed down. In addition, there are more accidents. We have just buried our tenth casualty. It's always tractors or rockfalls in the galleries, and you can never establish exactly who is responsible.

The "township" is filling up. Some of the men dismissed from Tignes have been lucky enough to find work here. We are at last going to open the recreation center, with games, music, reading, etc. But I wonder if we shall find enough good will to get it really going? We'll see this winter. Louis and Anna, former Youth Hostel leaders, have come to join me here for a few months. Their presence and their friendship are very precious to me. They will be able to help in developing the friendships I have already made here, and hence the living conditions of the worksite. With the calm that comes with the holiday season we get a real impression of living in an isolated beehive, but no less humming for that.

At the beginning of August we had a meeting of the twelve or thirteen priest-workers hereabouts, which was also attended by the Archbishop of Chambéry, Father A., and the Abbé H. It was one of our best meetings, and it looks as though our problems are now causing very little trouble for our bishops. We plan to have three days of recollection with them and two theologians at All Saints. It will surely be a good step forward.

I, like many others, really feel that the priest-workers are slowly taking their place in the contemporary world and that despite the noise and fuss made about us in the last few months,* we are taking root at the heart of the life and struggles of the workers. Many questions that still caused difficulties a few months ago, such as our participation in Union activities, are now accepted all round. As for living the life we lead with faith, I can't see how we could carry on for a single day without cleaving to it ever more firmly. With the help of your prayers, the ground is being cleared day after day, and I can't ask more of Our Lord.

Goodbye for now. I am with you with all my heart, and asking God to lead us all by the hand.

Cornimont,
September 29, 1952

Very dear Sister. Yesterday was the solemnity of St. Theresa. Soon we shall be having the feast of the little St. Theresa, then of the big one. This amounts to saying that I will be thinking about you a great deal in the days to come. Today I am thinking especially of Mother, with whom I'm spending 48 hours—a headlong escape from my worksite.

Don't be cross with me for writing so little. My circulars must have explained to you how little free time I have. I haven't forgotten the days I spent last September at your convent. . . . Everything has been providential, and all I can

---

* Henri is alluding to events of the previous spring which had again drawn attention to the priest-workers. At a demonstration of the Mouvement de la Paix (Movement for Peace) in Paris on May 18, two of them, together with hundreds of demonstrators, had been manhandled by the police. The press got very excited about it, and controversy broke out between Mgr. Feltin and the prefect of police, M. Baylot, who accused the two priest-workers of lying.

do is to ask you to thank Christ with me. I feel I'm in exactly the right place at my worksite, although poor indeed for representing the Church of Christ in the midst of 600 workers. Our bishops are more and more convinced that our presence is necessary. . . .

Everybody here at home in Cornimont wants to be remembered to you warmly—including Mother, who encloses this photograph of Our Lady of Peace, who is now protectress of the village, and including my godmother, who will be 86 the day after tomorrow. Andrée, Pierre, and the children left here three weeks ago.

I'm sending a view of my village; it's odd, but I haven't the faintest feeling of being in a remote corner. We need so little to fill a solitude and bring a whole world to life. . . .

IX

The Second Strike
at Isère-Arc
(1952–1953)

AFTER the holiday, the worksite filled up again to capacity
for completing the work on the dam. In October, 1952,
Henri's life was largely made up of his ten or eleven hours of
daily work, his union activities, and his efforts to broaden
the cultural outlook of his workmates by means of the new
recreation room.

The second winter at Notre-Dame-de-Briançon was a
time of privilege for the priest-workers on the dams; Cardinal
Liénart, patron of the Mission of France, had taken over responsibility for them, in co-ordination with the bishops of
the dioceses concerned.

After trips by two priest-workers to Paris and Lille, and a
day's meeting in Chambéry with three priest-workers, the
bishop, and a theologian, the All Saints meeting referred to
by Henri took place from October 30 to November 2 at the
Dominican House at Saint-Alban-Leysse. It was attended by

all the priest-workers in the region, as well as one or two
from Paris. The program for the discussion included:

1. Situation of the world we are living in. Why in practice
   is it inhuman and areligious?
2. What is its place in God's design?
3. What is the place of the mission of the Church, and
   hence of the priest, within it?
4. The function proper to the priest. Why does he have
   to gain entrance into this world by work?
5. The special religious needs for priest-workers.

Henri Perrin wrote of it to a friend: "I am writing on my
return from three splendid days with fifteen priest-workers,
two bishops, and several theologians near Chambéry. It's
the third or fourth time that we've met together, and we look
with joy *at the length of the road already traversed. . . .*"

At this time the center and café at 151 boulevard de la
Gare in Paris had to close because of difficulties, and Henri
wrote: "It's surely true that the world of brotherhood will
not come tomorrow. Sometimes it's hard enough to see even
the promise of it. As his end drew near, Christ could hardly
see it either. Well, ours has collapsed in death, but we won't
cry over the team in XIII. God is waiting for us further on."

After a gap of three months, Henri wrote a collective
letter to his friends:

Notre-Dame-de-Briançon,
November 25, 1952

Very dear Everyone. It's a long time since I've given you a
sign of life. I want to write, but it's not easy to know just
what to say. Life goes on so simply and so fully that there's
nothing and everything to say at the same time.

I'm still at the worksite and still in my workshop drilling holes in iron. My union activity is engrossing, especially as I'm now both workers' representative and member of the Joint Production Committee. I am still the only Christian in the midst of a mass of men that now numbers more than 700—and always struggling with evil, the evil within myself, as well as the evil that overwhelms others in a thousand ways. But all things considered, it's a very healthy life both physically and morally, and what is human in man emerges sufficiently often (in friendship, and love, and the struggle for justice) to make one keep one's faith in God and go on trusting in his "image."

. . . In all this [intense union activity], life with the Church is not very visible. The only outward signs of it, apart from Mass, are the meetings with the other priest-workers and the bishops. I think the days we are going to have in Paris around December 6 and 7 will confirm the work we are now doing. The priest-workers see more and more clearly what their mission is, and the bishops understand. The link with the world of the workers can only be achieved at a price which would astonish and even scandalize eight out of ten of present-day Christians. If a bishop were one day to become a worker, which I gather is not impossible, it won't be long before he thinks and acts much like the rest of us.

I don't know whether I make myself clear. I would need much more space to provide details. The reason the desire to write to you came over me again just now was, among other things, because I was afraid I was going to have to tell you that Ben Said (known as "Blanchette" ["Whitey"]) had died. He's a huge Negro who has been a close friend of mine ever since the strike, who calls everyone "my brother," and he has only just managed to survive being crushed by a landslide at the worksite.

Goodbye for now, for I must stop. I haven't forgotten you, and may God keep you all.

P.S. Louis and Anna are still here with me. Louis' finger is not yet better. Anna is managing the co-operative splendidly. They are invaluable.

Notre-Dame-de-Briançon,
December 30, 1952

Very dear Friends. I shall be writing even fewer letters this new year. May God keep all our hearts at peace and give peace to all. I have no other wish.

Now for news. Earlier in the month I spent ten days in Paris for two meetings—the priest-workers and the Central Committee of the firm. The latter meeting led to my being treated ferociously as a "Jesuit" by a managing director, and I could see that the others were literally wild with rage. Far from burning our bridges, however, it has led to wage adjustments as of January 6 that are going to cost the firm some four million francs. That will do instead of the bonus for the end of the year. The dispute about the concrete workers has been settled at last, after eight months of plugging away at their claim.

Otherwise, life on the worksite is very calm at present. Many of the men have gone off for the New Year holiday, and fresh faces crop up every day. There has been another period of hiring, and we are now 800, despite the fact that when things began, accommodation was planned for only 300. So you can imagine the billeting problems we have. In spite of this constant expansion, the union is now sufficiently strong to unite the whole worksite and create an atmosphere of trust and friendship. The recreation center now has ping-pong and jujitsu clubs, and we're making up a skiing team. In this way we're trying to "make things human." But there's still the question of unemployment, especially for the North Africans. They obviously won't find work either in France or Africa.

Louis and Anna and I spent Christmas with the secretary of the area union. I went to midnight Mass in the village church with his wife. It was a poor Mass, almost as poor as that night in Bethlehem—as poor, in any case, as the hearts of many of us, weighed down by so many things. The truth is that Christmas is not far from the cross; people will say that that doesn't get you anywhere and isn't funny. But all the same it gets you quite a long way if you have faith and believe in the Father's love.

One big change. I'm not drilling holes any more! I've again taken the place of the welder in the forge, and my foreman sees me using the blowtorch without stopping me. Quite an event! Louis will be leaving us soon to prepare for their move. Anna will stay on until she absolutely has to go back to Paris. . . .

In early January, 1953, there were two more fatal accidents on the worksite, both to North Africans.

To Paul G.

February 21, 1953

. . . I heard that you've been rather ill this winter. I wish you could breathe the air of these worksites. Physically it's healthy, except for the tunnel. Morally it's no worse than Paris.

But all the same it's a hell of a mess. Mankind seems to me more and more chaotic every day. What an age it seems since I left the seminary, when everything seemed so simple and "ordered," and laws were laws....

Since then I have come across men, and every day I discover more about myself.

To A.J.S. (One of his Youth Hostel friends)

February 21, 1953

... I've heard echoes of your Monday meetings [of the Paris priest-workers]. It would be surprising if there weren't any difficulties. Sufficient for the day. Our Lord is steering the boat.

We had a meeting of our team three weeks ago. We are now rather more dispersed, but we are going to spend Easter together at Thonon.

I'm not giving you much worksite news. I'll be writing a collective letter as soon as possible, and I'll send the third of our worksite bulletins. But briefly, we've reached the climax of the work; in three weeks the tunnel will be through, after which the men will start leaving, although there's still a year's work to be done. The union is booming; out of 950 workers, more than 600 have already joined. The boys are full of trust. But there's hardly any time to get to know one another and make friends.

But slowly, lots of things are happening.

Anna is now leaving, after eight full and valuable months here. Which only goes to show what scope there is among us for women of good will, and in many different ways.

Good night. I'm loyally with you and with everyone who's carrying on the mission in arrondissement XIII.

The little periodical referred to was called the "Journal de la Chute," and in its April, 1953, issue it described the completion of the tunnel under Mont-Bellachat (7,000 feet). It was a considerable technical achievement. When the two tunnels met, each about four miles long, the miscalculation at the juncture amounted to only 11 inches. Henri Perrin, however, was more concerned about impending unemployment. "Alas, this is the last worksite," he wrote in the "Journal." "We are being laid off. Three years ago, 40,000 workers were employed in public works. Now we are 9,000. Three months from now we may be only 3 or 4,000." Henri also wrote about the achievements of the union in the course of the past months:

The union brought a case before the court at Moutiers concerning a worker, Pantaric, who was dismissed six months ago. The evidence, heard in January, led to an important victory. On March 22 the magistrate ordered the firm to pay 160,000 francs indemnity, damages, and interest to Pantaric, as well as costs, for its "culpable irresponsibilty" and wrongful dismissal. This victory will make the management think twice before dismissing a worker in future.

In January the workers' representatives organized a collection for the family of our workmate Kadjetit, brutally killed on January 6. Some 320 men contributed to the collection, and the sum realized totalled 217,000 francs—an average of 700 francs per man.

We are also glad to report that a collection made by the union at the time of the distribution of bonuses for tunnel completion amounted to over 220,000 francs. With this sum and the one collected at Aiguebelle, the union council intends to buy a machine for copying all the documentation

that the worksite needs, as well as a small motorcycle for our
secretary, Rochaix, who until now has been wasting much
time going around by train and bus. Can you imagine someone permanently employed by the bosses going about by
train and bus?

Notre-Dame-de-Briançon,
April 1, 1953

My very dear Sister. Thank you for your letter of February
15. I can't blame you for writing so little, because my silence
has been just as great as yours, but I want you to get a letter
for Easter.

Don't worry; I have absolutely no fears regarding your constant thoughts of me and prayers for me; I know how much
you keep me going. And I would like to say a special thank
you to the sisters and novices who are helping us specially.
The autumn and winter have been calm and encouraging,
but now there seem to be clouds on the horizon once again.
God alone knows the ways along which He will lead our
workers' mission, which has begun and which will go on
whatever anyone says. For one day, either through us or
through others, God will make Himself known to these millions of men who have never experienced his love. For our
part, we are merely preparing the way, from afar and in the
dark. Others will follow . . .

Now for news, as you ask. Our life on the worksite goes
on without any great changes, but a thousand-odd incidents
to fill it. With evening Mass and our fairly regular priest-
worker meetings, the hundreds of problems that arise every
day with my workmates bring me into the presence of God.
Opportunities are not lacking. As to your question about
whether we've managed to get the recreation center going,

alas we have hardly any time to think of it. We can hardly ever find a free moment from our work problems (constant disputes about wages, about respect for our liberties, about impending unemployment), and when we do, we are caught up in personal problems, such as the jobless North Africans, family difficulties, and so forth. In the last four months there have been 900 of us at Notre-Dame-de-Briançon, and in all, nearly 2,000 working on the Isère-Arc project. The whole worksite life revolves around and is expressed by the union life; so the people I see are mostly responsible union people. In practice, I am the most responsible worker on the site, and nearly everyone shows complete trust in me. This is the most impressive, and at the same time the heaviest, side of our life as priest-workers. Many of the men show unlimited affection, which with some of them turns into deep friendship, in which we find all that is best in ourselves.

To give you an example of the sort of problems we are up against: As a result of the 1952 strike, we obtained, among other things, an agreement for a bonus of 60 million francs, of which half had to be paid when the tunnel was through, if this occurred before July, 1953. We got through last week, three months ahead of schedule, so 30 million was distributed within 36 hours at the canteen door. Now you must realize that on pay night some of the boys here are always drunk. I therefore put out a special appeal for dignity, which the workmates applauded. And I was really amazed to see that, in a worksite literally deluged with one-thousand-franc notes, there was not a single drunk in the canteen for two successive nights. On Saturday we held an enormous banquet (1,600 places), and I can't tell you how moved I was to be the only priest and at the same time the man who represented the 1,200 workers present. After the banquet

there were a lot of silly fights among the men. I and a few
others stood by to separate them, calm them down, and
bathe bleeding faces. Then, with the help of another workmate, I had to look after a young North African who was
having a nervous breakdown. And so on. Those particular
days were exceptional, but there's always something. How
in the world could I want to leave these men for the kids of
the parish club?

So everything's all right here. Physically I'm feeling marvelous. Morally, I'm beginning to show signs of moods and
lack of being at everyone's disposal, which must be a sign of
age.

As for other news, Mother seems to be well, although she
gets depressed at times. Poor Mother, she's now going to
have other worries with the news that my sister is going to
have another baby. You may have heard this already. It
weighs heavily on us all, because Andrée is showing signs
of fatigue and she'll need to be cared for in every possible
way. I've planned to spend more than half my holiday with
her, beginning at the end of July. So I haven't a moment for
the Vosges—at most a quick visit to Mother in September,
like last year. Don't hold this against me.

I must stop now, because I've suddenly thought I must
get off a line to Mother this evening without fail. So good
night, dear Lucie. Tomorrow, Holy Thursday, I know you'll
be thinking about us especially. On Easter Sunday there's a
meeting with the other priest-workers near Grenoble. May
God protect us.

Henri Perrin numbered among his friends an employer,
R.D., who, as the following letter suggests, sometimes tried
to point out to him that good employers did exist:

Ascension, 1953

... I quite agree with what you say about misunderstandings due to lack of contact. I'm sure this must be true for you and a certain number of others. But daily experience forces one to realize that one often has to contend with people who have no scruples whatever and all too many means for laying you low. Here's the most recent little example I've just experienced. Last year our managing director signed a declaration saying: "Ascension Day is a holiday; in future there will be no work on that day." But yesterday, at 11 in the morning, he had the cheek to telephone his foremen, saying that tomorrow will be a normal working day. And so on. I'm sorry to say I'm beginning to get used to it. He may be a particularly bad example, yet he isn't a bad man. Nearby, with D., it's worse still; and at the other end of our hole it's no better.

I shall be going to Paris around July 10 for the firm's Central Committee meeting. There, too, I foresee serious clashes. For instance, the doctor: he comes once a week to a worksite with 900 workers, and there's no health visitor, although there would be an enormous amount for her to do. ... You must realize that I'm saying all this without any unpleasant feelings and even without bitterness.

The events leading up to the second strike, which broke out on June 16, 1953, are best described in a collective letter:

Notre-Dame-de-Briançon,
May 13, 1953

... There's nothing particularly new. Life goes on at the worksite, but it's slowing down. No large-scale dismissals yet, but the boys are going off in driblets. Of the eleven

priest-workers in the whole of the dam enterprise, I am the
only one left still working on the dam. The others are getting
new jobs round about, but with difficulty. In view of our
worksite's folding up, we have to be more watchful over our
union life. Never a day passes without some friction with
the boss; never a fortnight without our being forced to
show our dissatisfaction by a work stoppage. Union life is
becoming more and more the operative point in the workers'
consciousness. More and more one is obliged to listen to,
love, and wrestle with one's workmates, and they are grateful
and responsive. But for all that, I don't want to play the part
of a judge. My life from many points of view is still poor,
humble, obscure, and sorrowful. The redemption has to be
like that.

June 10

More news. First of all, we had our thirteenth fatal accident on May 27. A foreman had his chest crushed by a tractor. It happened that I was at the hospital when he died, and
so lived through those hours intimately with his family, then
officiated at the funeral at Moutiers in very moving circumstances. Nearly the whole worksite attended. The responsibility of the management for the lack of safety precautions
was flagrant. I felt obliged to say something about it at the
graveside—briefly, but it went home.

At the same time I was anticipating an event which soon
followed. A list of dismissals appeared on June 2 which included my name. And since that date this has become the
main preoccupation of us all; all my mates think, and rightly,
that this has been done deliberately, and they're saying, "If
you go, we might as well pack up too, because there'd be no
more defense for us on the worksite."

We set things going by beating the boss on his own ground, by creating legal conditions which force him to keep me on. As he seems to want to play at being deaf, the workers downed tools for an hour on Saturday. This token strike was intended to make him think things over. The workers also held a general meeting at which they decided on a total strike, if necessary, to force the management to keep me on. Then we sent the management a long memorandum, on which the Joint Production Committee will have to decide on Thursday. We are convinced that management hasn't a leg to stand on legally, either over my dismissal or over dismissals in general. I think things will turn out all right. If it so happens that it is absolutely impossible to keep me on, the boys intend to ask me to stay and guarantee my wages.

There's another thing I'd like to talk about at length with you, and that's the death of Jacquot, found in the Seine ten days ago. We'll never know what happened. The only thing that matters to us is the suffering Jacquot underwent, and it frightens me to realize how terribly alone we all are in our struggles. We must try to do our best to break through loneliness, which is the thing most opposed to God. But it has to be admitted that in spite of appearances, we are often still far from doing all we could. . . .

June 14

Up to date, things don't seem to be going too well regarding the dismissals. The meeting of the Joint Production Committee produced a categorical refusal by the boss to change his attitude. Yesterday, a visit by the union secretary to the Labor Inspectorate failed to come up to our expectations. The Inspectorate is itself in a stew about the procedure

to follow in cases of collective dismissals. We have only three
more cards to play. The first, the resignation of the acting
representatives, has already been played, but the boss has
not yet put his card on ours; the second is that of the conciliation commission; and the third and last is a strike. Pro-
visionally, we have decided on a strike, to begin next Thursday morning.

My morale is fine, all the more so as today we had a
splendid meeting with the other priest-workers. Still, these
endless days of squabbling are tiring.

You all know my affection for you and how I trust in your
prayers.

A general strike began on June 16. This second strike was
not as long as the 1952 one; it lasted twenty-two days. It was
also less complex. Yet it was harder, the management was
tougher, and personal feelings ran higher.

As in 1952, both the provincial and Parisian press followed
the activities of the strikers, and there was generous response
to the appeals made by the solidarity committee.

Its causes couldn't have been more clear and just. This is
how they were announced to the people:

After sixteen months, the workers on worksite B., Isère-
Arc, Notre-Dame-de-Briançon, are again embarking on an
unrestricted strike.

They are forced to do so by the stubborn obstinacy of a
boss whose incompetence becomes more manifest every day.

They do so only after having forewarned the management,
throughout ten days, of their obligation to strike if their
rights were not respected.

Their rights? First and foremost these are concerned with

respect for the rules and regulations governing dismissals. The people, after the workers themselves, will be astonished to learn that collective dismissals have been going on for two months without the authorization of the Inspectorate of Labor, and bypassing its demands. Special concern is felt over the dismissal of workers' representatives, notably the secretary of the Joint Production Committee, our workmate Perrin, whom the boss wants to be rid of, without any authorization and against the will of the workers whose voice should be heard.

Their rights? These concern also an increase in basic wages....

Their rights? These concern also small matters of bonuses and grave matters of security to safeguard the lives of the workers....

The strike has started. It is a struggle against a policy of low wages and unemployment. That is why we appeal to your sympathy, and tomorrow, if necessary, to your solidarity.

We had everyone's sympathy in 1952; we have it again today. Strengthened by our rights and your support, WE SHALL WIN AGAIN.

An account of the strike was given by Maurice Verdy, in typical Communist language, in the final issue of the "Journal de la Chute." As it gives a useful over-all picture, it should be quoted here:

Long shall I remember the splendid strike of last June when the management had violated in all hypocrisy the law concerning the Joint Production Committee by illegally dismissing our secretary, Comrade Perrin. In general assembly all the workers voted for an unrestricted strike to

defend both the union rights, and the best man among us—
the man whom all the workers loved and respected for his
uprightness and sincerity, the man who succeeded in uniting
all our workmates on the worksite in our own union. I myself
am rather ashamed today, for at first I used to reproach him
with being too soft with the management. What a lesson he
has taught me since, for not one of us has endured such
humiliations as he from the central management in Paris,
where men like Guillot and Parot had the cheek to push him
around and expel him from the meeting of the Joint Production Committee!

I can still see our strike pickets and the motorized police
with machine guns on their shoulders coming up to us and
saying: "You on strike to defend a priest! I can't understand
it." And when we explained that the union includes men of
all political and religious views, they went off, shrugging their
shoulders. Poor motorized police, one day you too will understand, and your machine guns will be at the service of the
working class, that is to say, at the service of France. I can
see our North African comrades, who were magnificent in
this strike, the ones who were on picket duty with me and
whom the police threw out and humiliated, although among
them were ex-soldiers of the last war. One of them said to
me sadly, "On my identity card they say I'm French, and
the police have just told me that only the French can stay
here and that I'd better make off or they'd put me in prison."
I thought of Jean Jaurez crying out at the injustice of the
words "Liberty, Equality, Fraternity."

In spite of all police and management pressure on the
workers, we were as united after twenty days of strike as on
the first. An old hand in the firm who hadn't much faith in
our movement said, "There's no fighting against B.; there's

no fighting against a man like Guillot; he made our strike at
Peyrat-le-Chateau fizzle out, and he'll do the same here."
But, comrades, B. was beaten at Briançon in June and July,
1953, by the will of the workers. Let it serve as an example.

I still remember our boss on the eve of the strike. He
looked so sure of himself as he said, "It isn't worth while
your going on strike, you've lost already." He seemed strong;
but as soon as comrade Lopez had got the representatives'
signatures for an unrestricted strike, I saw his face suddenly
change. And when, on July 6, we met again at Albertville to
come to an agreement, I remember how this big boss seemed
to lose his man's dignity when confronted with the arguments of our comrades Granet, Rochaix, Perrin, Lopez, and
all our other representatives. You could feel that he had
lost a battle. . . .

We went back to work in fine fettle and kept comrade
Perrin as permanent representative. But once again there
was trouble. The management at Briançon started man-
euvers to expel him from the "township": they had his bed
taken away, and appealed to the courts. Nothing happened.
He stayed with us. We were stronger when we faced the
management. We were more respected. Our conditions of
work were noticeably improved, and so were our wages, because the boss knew that all the workers were with us.

June 27, 1953

Dear Everyone. I am writing a few lines because I imagine
you may be uneasy until you know how far we have got in
our new strike, declared against our will.

Last Tuesday, on the advice of the Labor Inspectorate
itself, the Committee sent me to Paris to tell the press and

the powers that be about our problems and force a discussion on the management. From the beginning, the bosses' tactics have been to avoid all discussion and try to hire workers living here and there in the neighborhood. This maneuver is well known for breaking strikes, and by Saturday a large number of foremen and fifteen workers had returned to work. The general manager himself spent all Friday going from door to door and using all the obvious forms of pressure, but we were able to check him; our militant representatives followed in his footsteps, local strike committees were formed, and at 5 o'clock this Monday morning the management, although it had already announced the return to work for today in the press, received a bitter rebuff—not a single worker turned up.

In Paris I went to see Le Monde, Combat, La Croix, and so on, and was able to have a 45-minute talk with Bacon, the Minister of Labor. He admits that the firm is in the wrong and says he is ready to adopt sanctions against them. But there is no law that forces the boss to come to terms; only administrative, political, or economic pressures can force him to agree to discuss and give way.

Of course an unrestricted strike is a very grave matter, especially when one is oneself, so to speak, the principal object of dispute. But I am so backed up and encouraged by nearly all the men, and in such a wholehearted and splendid way, that it has become relatively easy. The strike is being led strongly and determinedly by some thirty boys who weren't here last year. A lot of our workmates have gone home and will come back only when they receive notice.

I trust in your friendship and prayers, and again send you all my affectionate feelings.

Communiqué, July 2, 1953

... *Following conversations between the Strike Committee and the Prefecture, the Prefect of Savoy has ordered a meeting of the conciliation commission this morning. It is to be hoped that the management of B. will give up its attempt to break the strike by means of icy silence and the brute force of money, and will consent to discuss. The strikers are endeavoring to bring to this meeting proposals for a settlement, which should put an end to the dispute. If the management persists in refusing discussion, the strikers can only become tougher, supported by the sympathy and solidarity of all.*

On Thursday, July 2, on the order of the Prefect of Savoy, the meeting of the conciliation commission took place, and conciliation was proposed on the following bases:

1. Unconditional cancellation of the dismissals made on June 2.
2. The fixing of a 48-hour week for work underground.
3. A free work timetable for the workshops, on condition that there will be no more dismissals as long as there is more than a 40-hour week.
4. Recommendation to the firm to respect the legislation now in force regarding dismissals.
5. Recommendation to the firm that it should re-employ at Aiguebelle the men dismissed.

The management did not accept these terms, but a modification of them, as Henri Perrin recounts:

... *There's to be no revision of basic wages. ... But the workers dismissed on June 2 are to be re-employed at Aigue-*

*belle, except for two North Africans and . . . me! There's also
to be some good bonus increases, guaranteed up to the shutdown of the worksite. . . . This morning at the general assembly I had to use all my eloquence to convince the boys
that it really wasn't desirable to continue the dispute just
to achieve my reintegration into the work. Thus I won't be
taking up my workshop duties any more, but I shall continue with my union activities, and assure the continuation
of my job as representative and secretary—if the boss doesn't
put spokes in the wheels, which he seems determined to do.*

*. . . So we turn another page! Today I'm breathing sighs
of relief. The struggles ahead will not be fun, but I have the
full support of all our workmates and of the union. Without
them, as you can imagine, I wouldn't stay here another day.*

This is the text of the motion the workers voted this morning, which has been handed to the boss: "The workers have
unanimously decided that the representative and secretary
of the Joint Production Board, Perrin, will remain on the
worksite and shall by every means continue to carry out the
mandate which they have entrusted to him and which is
guaranteed by law."

There's the working class for you.

The men went back to work on July 9.

During the last eight months at the worksite a very petty
underground war was carried on. The management tried to
get back Henri's mattress, which "went with his wages."
("They do things in a grand style at B.," the Under-Prefect
was reported as saying when told about it.) The only mis-
fortune was that Henri Perrin had not been sleeping on
that mattress for the last ten months. But the management

considered that its honor had been satisfied and that Perrin was "off the premises."

The *Journal de la Chute* also recounts that at the end of the strike a collection was made "to guarantee Perrin's livelihood after he had wrongfully and illegally been dismissed by the firm, and to date has realized 80,000 francs at Notre-Dame-de-Briançon. Some of the worksites have not yet been approached and the collection is continuing. The union council will decide how this sum is to be used."

To stabilize the situation, Henri was accepted as pay clerk of the social security pay office at Chambéry. He carried out this task with enormous care, and it enabled him to join even more closely in the life of his workmates and to get a grasp of their personal and family problems.

The "Journal" announced this:

Social security: the union has asked comrade Perrin to open an office on the worksite at Notre-Dame-de-Briançon. This means that henceforth you can hand over your insurance card to Perrin, who will see whether your papers are in order and will see that they reach the paying office; normally, payments will be made directly by Perrin in accord with the allowance sent by the paying office. This will allow you to overcome most of your difficulties arising from incomplete or incorrectly completed papers and will enable you to be paid on the spot a few days after you have handed in your papers, thus saving the cost of journeys to Chambéry and the loss of time involved. . . . For the time being the pay office will be open at union headquarters in the "township" on three days a week, Tuesday, Thursday, and Saturday, from 10 A.M. till midday, and from 2 P.M. to 4 P.M.

Henri Perrin considered that he owed the union 40,000 francs for the wages it provided him during this period. Although the sum was given him unconditionally, he intended to return it as soon as he won the case he had brought up against the management for illegal dismissal. But the firm did not give in so easily. It appealed the decision.

When the Inspector of Labor proposed extending the period of office of representatives until the shutdown of the worksite, the firm contested this and demanded that new representatives, including those of the Joint Production Committee, should be elected. The *Journal de la Chute* commented in November, 1953:

"Of course we shall be nominating Perrin, as in the eyes of the law he is still employed by the firm, and we have excellent reasons to demand that the law should be applied. It is odd to see how the management is concerned about some laws but not others. Guillot wants us to hold these elections to get rid of Perrin. But there will be a plebiscite in which we shall again express our will to keep him with us."

The development of events is described in the "Journal" for January, 1954:

"Our readers have already been informed of the disputes between employees and the management. Despite the strikes of 1952 and 1953, the management still does not consider itself beaten. It is doing what many managements are doing at the moment, summarily getting rid of workers' leaders who are most active.

"Hence, last June the management tried to make use of collective dismissals to get rid of the secretary of the Joint Production Committee, our comrade Perrin. This maneuver immediately led to a strike and then developed into the *affaire* Perrin. The firm brought the case before the arbitration court at Moutiers. The judge, in his first judgment, ordered the firm to put Perrin's name on the election roll both as voter and candidate, and, in a second judgment, 'to pay Perrin his wages up to date, to take him back into employment, or, failing this, to pay him 300,000 francs compensation.' As the firm appealed, it has not yet been obliged to carry out this ruling but it will soon be forced to.

"Moreover, after a long period of hesitation, the Inspectorate of Labor brought a case against the firm for breaking laws and hindering the proper functioning of the Joint Production Committee. This case, which has been added to the one brought up by the union, is going to bring the owner before the correctional court and, we hope, sentence him to a fine and possibly prison, as well as to paying of compensation.

"On December 7 the Inspectorate of Labor for the hydroelectric worksites in the Alps wrote to the management: 'I am obliged to remind you that the dismissal of M. Perrin was rejected on June 25, 1953, by the Director of Labor in Savoy.

" 'The eviction of M. Perrin from the committee of your establishment is, therefore, irregular and constitutes a hindrance to the regular functioning of this committee. Such hindrance is punishable by a fine and imprisonment by Article 24 of Disposition No. 45280 of February 22, 1945. Imprisonment becomes obligatory if the offense is repeated in the course of the year. I have no option but to urge you to reconsider your position in the matter.' "

The firm lost all the cases in which it was involved.

X

The End of the Priest-Worker Experiment

(1953 – 1954)

From July, 1953, on, interest in the Isère-Arc dispute was largely eclipsed by the drama which was soon to rock the Church from top to bottom and bring the priest-worker movement in its existing form to an end.

Henri Perrin was present at the national meetings of the priest-workers held in Paris on July 13–14. A great uneasiness as to their future was already apparent. The recall by Mgr. Delay in May of the three Marseilles priest-workers seemed to forecast wider measures.

Meanwhile, France was in the grip of widespread labor troubles. On the night of July 14, Henri went to a meeting in the Place de la Nation with a delegation from Isère-Arc and witnessed the savage intervention of the police which resulted in seven dead and forty wounded.

The month of August, 1953, remains in everyone's memory as a month of massive strikes—such as there had not been since November, 1947. At a moment of great hope, when it looked as if the recall of Parliament was inevitable, the millions of workers felt utterly let down by the behind-the-scenes agreements negotiated by C.F.T.C. and F.O.* leaders on the one hand, and M.R.P. ministers and their colleagues on the other. These agreements upset many of the Christians, and not unnaturally the priest-workers echoed this dissatisfaction, which spread far beyond circles influenced by the Communist Party and the C.G.T.

However, the crisis for the priest-workers themselves, and for the working-class Christian militants who were associated with them and supported them, is the main theme of Henri's last letters. It was a crisis in which, as Henri felt, the Catholic hierarchy showed its fear of the new world that he was representing and defending at the very moment when he was feeling his deepest communion with it. The following are a few dates showing the course of events:

July 27.   Periods in factories were forbidden to seminarians.

August 29.   Superiors of religious orders were asked to recall their priest-workers.

September 6.   Closing of the seminary of the Mission de France at Limoges.

September 23.   After similar meetings at Toulouse and Lyons, the Papal Nuncio handed over to twenty-six Bishops and Superiors of religious orders who had been summoned to Paris, instructions from Rome concerning priest-workers. Cardinals Liénart, Feltin, and Gerlier decided to go to Rome to state their case.

September 25.   The Catholic daily, *La Croix*, argued that the priest-worker experiment should be perfected and

* *Confedération française de Travailleurs Chrétiens* (Christian Trade Unions) and *Forces Ouvrières* (Socialist Trade Unions).

continued (it took the same line in two further articles, on October 11 and 13).

October 4. Four hundred militant members of the "Action Catholique Ouvrière" (Workers' Catholic Action) began a series of meetings in Paris that reflected the growing feelings of anxiety among Christian workers throughout the whole of France.

October 6. François Mauriac, well-known Catholic writer, said: "The priest-workers are our pride. . . . We cannot even conceive of a day when they are no longer there."

October 13. Bishops with priest-workers in their dioceses, summoned to Paris before the departure of the three Cardinals for Rome, found their meeting forbidden.

October 14, 15, 16. The Assembly of the Cardinals and Archbishops of France. No communiqué was issued. There was no statement about the priest-workers.

The left-wing Catholic periodical, *Jeunesse de l'Église,* was condemned.

October 31. The priest-workers of Paris wrote to Cardinal Feltin: "To forbid union activity for priest-workers is tantamount to forbidding them to take part in working-class life."

November 4, 5, 6. The three French Cardinals in Rome. In the following days there was widespread press comment in Rome. The Cardinals communicated to their priest-workers what they had brought back from Rome.

November 15. This was now made public in the following declaration: "After ten years of existence, the priest-worker experiment as it has developed up till now cannot continue.

"The Church therefore demands:

1. That priest-workers should be specially chosen by their Bishops.
2. That they should receive a solid formation in doctrine.
3. That they should devote only a *limited time* to work.
4. That they should leave temporal responsibilities to laymen.
5. That they should play their part in the life of the parish.

November 25. The bishops asked the priest-workers to give up their temporal commitments and quietly leave their unions.

Notre-Dame-de-Briançon,
November 28, 1953

Very dear Friends. I am receiving some really brotherly letters from you, but I haven't answered because of lack of time. I hope each one of you individually will forgive me. But things have now become too black for me to fail to respond to your friendship any longer.

The main reason you write to me is because of the current difficulties at the very heart of the Church. There is no denying that in the past two months we have been sifted like sand, and life has been made hard for us. For more than a month I have been spending my Sundays with the team of priest-workers in this outfit, and I spent one Sunday in Paris with representatives of various other groups of priest-workers. We know almost word for word—and far better than the press—the reactions of the Bishops and Cardinals toward us and the details of the steps taken in Rome. It is quite clear that they had already decided on the unconditional suppression of the priest-workers a month ago; it is clear, too, that the situation was saved to outward appear-

ances by the Cardinals. But everything is still very con-
fused and ambiguous. The statute proposed by the hierarchy
through the press unfortunately showed an almost total
ignorance of the workers' world—both of its problems and of
its position in relation to the Church. And this is very serious. We cannot fail to be grateful to our bishops for their
concern for our lives as priests, but the number one problem
for them, as for us, should by rights be that of the Church's
relationship with the workers' world. Now, things like asking us to work for a few hours every day, or to keep out of
the workers' movement—and hence the trade union movement—or to maintain a link with the parish, involve a misunderstanding of the basic conditions of our life as workers
and of any genuine worker's life.

It is this difference of view which puts us in difficulties
with the hierarchy, and we can't keep quiet about it because
it would remove all truth from the Church's mission in the
world of the workers. And, let's face it, it is this point which
makes ordinary Christian circles—including the hierarchy
—uneasy, because they want to shut their eyes to the problems raised by a genuine meeting between the Church and
the workers' world. I don't really want to say any more at
the moment. In addition, even my present preoccupations
as a worker show how impossible it is for us to live in the
workers' world without taking up all its problems, including
its political ones.

As you know, I'm still living at the Isère-Arc worksite. I
appealed to the arbitration tribunal as early as July, but my
case was only heard in the middle of November. My lawyer
is an old union lawyer from Paris, Maître Boitel, and we
prepared my defense together. It was the first time in his
life that he had defended a priest.

For a whole variety of reasons the judge wanted to come to a quick decision. But in fact he won't be doing so before next Friday, or even later. I am fully confident that the firm will be ordered either to take me on again (not much chance of that!) or to pay compensation. On Friday I shall also be busy defending other cases against the firm—one for unjustified withholding of part of the wages of a North African, the other the improper dismissal of a worker who, like me, was included in the dismissals of June 2. But my biggest job is pressing that the owner should be brought before the correctional court, on legal complaint of the Inspectorate of Labor. I have been confronted with the astonishing spectacle of an Inspector who has seen his decisions brushed aside during the past six months, and who has been insulted in various ways. He feels it is essential to take the case to court, and he drew up an official report against the owner three months ago. He has even been asked by the Minister of Labor himself to bring up the case, and yet he doesn't do so. We are convinced that this is due to pressure brought to bear on him by the Prefect, by the Minister of the Interior, and doubtless by the political circles supported by the owner. It is probably these very people who are denouncing us to the Vatican, either directly or through intermediaries.

. . . At lunchtime, when I was in the canteen, a worker asked me if I would "bless his wedding," and added that he would rather pay me 1,000 francs than someone else. This led to a long conversation about his marriage, and it became plain that I couldn't possibly marry him, because he wasn't really serious. They will be married by the parish priest at Salins; there has to be a religious marriage because of the girl's aunt, who is a nun. It's the classic situation; it has nothing to do with religion.

. . . I long to meet you all before the spring.

After the excitement and anxiety at the time of the Cardinals' journey to Rome and the very free comments in the press on their declaration, December was somewhat calmer. The priest-workers were waiting to see how the five points already quoted were going to be implemented, although they were apprehensive almost to the point of despair.

A number of the hierarchy spoke out in favor of their priest-workers. Thus, for instance, Mgr. Feltin, on December 1: "The whole world is preoccupied by the question of the priest-workers, as is shown by the letters that have come to Archbishop's House. The positive results of this kind of apostolate are obvious. Wherever there are priest-workers, the priestly influence has been effectively brought to bear, as is proved by the countless individuals and families who have returned to Christ because of it."

And Mgr. Chapoulie, Bishop of Angers, said much the same on Christmas Day: "We must never forget that the French clergy has had the honor of being the first to be involved in this search for close and Christian contact with the working classes by sharing their work, their anguish, and their experiences."

Notre-Dame-de-Briançon,
December 20, 1953

My very dear Ones. Just a few lines to give you news before Christmas. You'll be wanting to know the results of the various court cases I have on my hands.

On December 4, the judge at Moutiers issued three judgments in our favor. In one he said that I was both an elector and eligible for election when the workers' representatives

are elected, and that my name should be included on the
electoral roll. Another judgment ordered the firm to reim-
burse a North African workmate for wages improperly with-
held—6,000 francs, plus 5,000 francs compensation, plus
costs. A third judgment declared my dismissal to be illegal
and void, and ordered the boss to pay me 300,000 francs
compensation. The boss immediately appealed. On December 10, when we had a new meeting of the central committee, the bosses dared to call in the police to make me
leave the hall. Two policemen asked me to go with them to
the police station, but when the officer saw my papers (a
letter from the Inspector of Labor, and the judgment of the
court at Moutiers), he apologized and said I could go back to
the meeting and lodge a complaint. I didn't much want to
do this, but felt I had to, so I asked the other representatives
to come out, and we all went back in together; the bosses
didn't bat an eye. Naturally this will become the subject of
a new court case, so the management now has four more
cases looming in front of it. In the end the light may
dawn. . . .

I don't want to say anything about the problem of the
priest-workers. One increasingly gets the impression, alas,
that churchmen draw back as soon as they reach the thresh-
old of the problems raised by the workers' world. And although they say kind words, which are often sincere, they
refuse really to involve themselves in the problems of the
workers' world along lines that would oblige them to revise
their alliances: it's impossible to live in the employers' world
and at the same time serve justice. We are all terribly
weighed down by the conviction that, behind the bishops'
solicitude for our priestly life, there lurks a political fear of
Communism and all sorts of pressures from the higher-ups.

One thing is certain: the voice of the poor is not listened to, and if you really do listen to it you come under suspicion. This is a sad thing to say just before Christmas, I agree, but Christmas brought hope to the night of the poor and of those who find it hard to hope. As long as we belong with them, we are in good company.

That's the company I wish for you, and it isn't difficult to come by it. You don't have to look around much; you just have to accept it and it comes by itself, just as God is there for anyone who turns to Him.

With all my wishes and my love.

The following are a few more significant dates:

December 28, 1953. The Society of Jesus recalled its priest-workers. Henri Perrin, who had long been a member of the Society and had many friends in it—and was well aware of the position occupied by the Jesuits in the Church —was inclined to see this measure as "the beginning of the end."

January 5, 1954. Mgr. Ancel said, "We are up against a missionary problem far deeper than anything that can be imagined."

January 19. After meeting in Paris, the bishops who had priest-workers under their jurisdiction sent to each individually a circular letter formulating their final decisions:

1. It was forbidden to do full-time work.
2. It was forbidden to belong to any organization whatever and accept the responsibilities this involved.
3. They should be reattached to some ecclesiastical community.
4. It was forbidden to form a team on the national level.

Notre-Dame-de-Briançon,
January 28, 1954

Very dear Everyone. I can't write to you without a word about this bombshell.

This will be brief. Now there are no more priest-workers. We heard the news on Saturday from Cardinal Liénart, who summoned us to Lille to tell us of all the decisions, and confirmed them afterward in writing. We received our funeral oration, "You have been splendid, thank you; now all you've got to do is to leave, under pain of excommunication." Liénart was too stunned to speak, and so were we.

I shall be leaving here at the end of February, although I'll have to come back in March for my court cases.

You probably won't be hearing from me again for some months. With God's help, I still believe in God, in Christ, and in the Church; but something has been broken which can't be mended.

Thank you for your prayers and affection.

Notre-Dame-de-Briançon,
January 28, 1954

Very dear Sister. No, I haven't forgotten you. If you knew how few letters I've written in the last two years through lack of time you would understand. And you're the first person I'm writing to since Saturday's bombshell. Please judge how devoted my affection is.

I haven't the heart to write at any length. Anyway, what can I say? Everything we've been doing for the last ten years has been repudiated and chucked away. All I can do is enclose my latest circular letters. Some of the things I say will distress you, but I wouldn't be sincere if I didn't say them.

Our bishops had to obey the Holy Office.

If the Holy Father felt he had to make a decision, it was because he was receiving requests for the creation of priest-workers from all over the world, as he himself told the Cardinals. I asked Cardinal Liénart why, with such grave things at stake, there had been no thought of sending a bishop to work for a few months, so that he could get genuine knowledge of the problem. The Cardinal agreed with us that the real drama is that in the present condition of the Church, it is not even thinkable for a bishop to go to work for a short time.

I don't want to go into a post-mortem. I'm hurting you, and I'll be hurting you again. But our hurt is nothing compared with that of the millions of workers who feel they have been abandoned and betrayed by the Church of Christ. No high-sounding words can alter the facts.

Pray that the priests of Christ will not reject the poor. We'll all have to give accounts of ourselves on the Gospel, and it is so easy to betray the Gospel.

I can only promise you one thing: I won't turn in revolt against the Church. But there are things that can no longer be done.

With deepest love. I thank you more than ever for your affection and prayers, and remember you in mine.

January 26. The bishops issued a communiqué. From now on priest-workers were to be "priests of the working-class mission." No further clarification was given.

January 27. Cardinal Feltin asked for prayers for "those who are particularly crucified by certain decisions."

February 3. The priest-workers broke their silence with a brief communiqué to their workmates. Henri Perrin, who was one of the seventy-eight priest-workers to sign the communiqué, explained his point of view in his last circular letter. The Catholic press reacted unfavorably to this communiqué, unaware that simultaneously each team had written a letter to its bishop and that the two were intended to appear together.

February 7. This and the following days were taken up with letters, appeals, meetings, and delegations of laymen calling on the bishops.

February 9. The three Dominican Provincials of France (that is, of Paris, Lyons, and Toulouse) were removed from office. Four eminent members of the Order, Fathers Chénu, Féret, Congar, and Boisselot were banished from Paris. As no explanation was given, it was supposed that the reason for these strong measures was that these men were well known for their sympathies with the priest-workers, and had given theological support to the current of missionary activity in France. Henri knew a number of them who had supported his mission in *arrondissement* XIII, and he suffered with them.

February 11. Cardinal Ottaviani, of the Holy Office, contrasted seeking after material bread to seeking after heavenly bread, and let it be known that one of the errors of the priest-workers was that they paid more attention to the first than the second.

A similar theme was taken up in an article in the *Osservatore Romano* of February 19, entitled "The misuses of charity."

February 16. An article by François Mauriac entitled "In favor of the new Concordat" caused considerable stir in Rome.

February 17. Questions asked in the Government by

MM. Michelet and Deixonne concerning the attitude of the Papal Nuncio caused a stir in Paris.

Mauriac argued: "It would be in the interests of the Church if one day she had to face an interlocutor who had rights other than keeping silence."

February 20 and 21.   Priest-workers from all over France held meetings at the Café de la Paix in Villejuif, near Paris, to discuss information, make decisions, and so on.

These were days of anguish. A splendid national team had been broken forever. Cornered by the "impossible choice," some of them submitted to the Church in a dark night of faith, with the hope that further discussions with the hierarchy might result in some revision of the official decision. Others, who felt unable to break the bonds they had forged with their workmates, continued to live under the usual conditions of the worker's life and accepted, in faith, the penalties already announced, ready to accept with obscure hope a long wait until they found a place in the Church with their fellow workers.

Henri, almost alone, made a desperate effort to evade the dilemma. He left his work, because the worksite closed down. But what was he going to do next? That remained an open question.

Notre-Dame-de-Briançon,
February 25, 1954

My Friends. I thought at first I wouldn't write. But things are too serious, and you'll be expecting to hear from me.

First, regarding my own situation: until this week, I felt sure I would have been able to leave the worksite even when it was still in full swing. Now I'm not so sure. I now feel that if I'd had to leave the boys at the height of the work and slip away like a thief or a traitor (because that's how the mass of workers would view it), I wouldn't have been able nor had the right to do it.

And this brings me to the special reason I wanted to write. At the beginning of next week the press will be revealing the brutal reality: some 50 priest-workers are staying on at their work, preferring excommunication to what seems to them a betrayal of the world of the poor.

In view of a position held by so many, it would be indecent and dishonest to raise cries of pride, lack of faith, Marxization, or whatever. The decision deserves respect; God alone can judge; the Church has the right and duty to take the measures it deems necessary; no sincere Christian can make accusations.

All I hope is that this should make us measure the extent to which Christian circles have always failed to take the problem of the workers seriously. Year after year, pious claptrap is doled out, and that's all. It's so sad to think of the letter the General of the Jesuits wrote in 1949, pinpointing the workers' world as the object of the Society's apostolate —and now look at the results! A mountain has given birth to a mouse. The middle class always has the Society's life forces at its disposal, so everything is more and more enclosed in a ghetto, as well as in a stupid form of anti-Communism. I could go on about this forever.

Some people have written that they were offended by the "Marxist-sounding" tone of our communiqué. First of all, if this was so, it only proves that this language is the language of the working world. We speak the language of the world we are in, and the language is in no way an offense to our faith, just as Saint Thomas talked the language of the Arabian philosophers, to the great scandal of his contemporaries. However it may seem, it is not a partisan language. True, it reflects the class struggle, but we live in the class struggle as we live in the war in Indo-China. If Christian circles were surprised by our communiqué, it only shows how far they are from the world of the workers. I feel that something would be achieved if present events provided the occasion for people to think honestly about the position of Christians regarding the workers' world. As things are now, there are social problems, as there are religious problems. My impression is that all the problems I tried to face between 1935 and 1945, and tried to put down in my little book, are still starkly with us. Now almost every page of my Diary is contradicted by events. The expressions that I was always using in those days, such as "Catholic ghetto" and "the desire to live frankly among other men"—to which I haven't given a thought in the last ten years—come back to me. One thing is certain: it is impossible that I should ever go back to the ghetto.

I will end by saying that I am firmly convinced that, in this business, obedience to the faith is not in question. The Church adopts the measures it thinks fit; it has the right, I say again. But one would have to be simple indeed to believe that good will can make up for everything, and that the deep and tragic gulf that separates the Church from the workers can be filled without terrible upheavals disturbing the Church and making it suffer as Christ did in his agony. Too many problems have now arisen, and the spirit of submission is not enough to solve them. When such problems come up in a man's conscience, his first duty to his conscience is not to evade them. And everyone knows that in the depths of his conscience, God is judging him.

Good night, my friends. I am not asking you to write to

me. I merely wanted to say what my friendship for you bids
me say. May God help us.

Extract from another letter sent to various people, including
Cardinal Liénart

. . . The works where I am employed are closing down. I
will have finished here on March 1. My act of obedience to
the Church of Christ will consist in not taking up work elsewhere as long as I have a priestly charge. For the moment, all
I am asking of the hierarchy is six months' leave. After a few
weeks' rest with friends, and then with my family, I would
like to live a retired life with M. le Curé of V. I am com-
municating this letter to Mgr. Jauffres, in whose charge I
was here, and to Mgr. Lamy, my bishop.

I have no desire to go back over all the things we have
told you and written you about the distress of millions of
souls, whether inside or outside the Catholic faith, who
through us had begun to discover the face of Christ in the
Church. Rome has decreed that it must all be wiped out. So
be it. . . .

But all the events of these recent months are fraught with
overwhelming consequences; too many things have been
done which are not God's work—done by us, alas, but also
by those who govern the Church.

Tomorrow the drama will continue in the consciences of
thousands of Christians, above all priests, and will be added
to the other burdens that are already heavy to bear.

On February 26 the worksite closed down, as the winter
ended. The "township" at Notre-Dame-de-Briançon was
emptied, and its relics left to rust in the rain. The hundreds

of French, Italian, Spanish, and North African workmates left to look for other work. They might be lucky, or they might not.

There is no need to try to describe what Henri felt as he said goodbye to his workmates of the past two years.

Only two more short notes of his have survived:

February 26, 1954

Very dear Sister. I feel I must send you these two letters. They will cause you suffering. But the very fact that I'm sending them will show you how deep my communion is with you. Besides, the measures leveled against the priest-workers make you suffer as much as us, and I know that you belong to the part of the Church that goes through Gethsemane most.

I have already had an answer from Mgr. Lamy, who willingly grants me six months' leave. Deeply yours.

March 27, 1954

Very dear Sister. I feel sure you will like this card. I hope it will join you in the joys of Easter after all the suffering my last letter must have caused you. But this suffering is very little compared with the suffering we can feel over the great divorce between the Church and the world of the workers. With us, or without us, or in spite of us, God will fill that gulf; if only we don't put too many spokes in the wheels. Very faithfully yours in prayer.

On October 25, 1954, there was an appalling telephone call.

On his way to the training center at Issy-les-Moulineaux, where, with the agreement of his bishop, he was completing a course as an electrician, Henri was killed on his motor bicycle.

No light was ever shed on the cause of the accident. There was no traffic. An astonished cyclist, a few yards ahead of him, was unable to explain what had happened. His skull was smashed, in spite of his helmet, and death was instantaneous.

The last eight months of his life are almost as mysterious as the circumstances of his death.

After the court hearing in the spring, which Henri eventually won, he took refuge in silence. He tried to bear his almost infinite distress alone, and avoided inflicting it on those whom he loved and who, until now, had been his confidants and companions. He kept apart; although, either directly or through intermediaries, he helped out a certain number of "brothers" in need. He kept up only with one or two of the families closest to him.

We must preserve complete respect for his silence and not attempt to break into the life of "God's unknown," as someone has referred to him. The few friends who saw him in the last weeks of his life have grounds to insist that the mystery be respected.

But it is mistaken to think that this silence must be an awkward one, as if the path he took condemned his whole way of life because it failed to lead in any visible way to joy and conviction. And it is even more mistaken to ask, "What would he have done if he had lived?" This question is not our business, and it would be hateful if it were asked in an effort to place him in one camp or the other, or turn him into the bone of contention he refused to be during this period.

It is true that Henri wanted to escape from the two days'

agony at Villejuif and the irreparable break between those who gave up work and those who went on with it.

It is true that he went on seeing both the former and the latter, not regularly, but when the occasion arose.

It is true that at the deepest level he questioned not *the* priesthood, but *his* priesthood, and that in October, the month of his death, he was considering asking to be laicized,* as he had every ground for thinking that, when his apprenticeship as an electrician was over, he would not get permission to work in a factory.

It is also true that he kept his letter appealing for laicization in his pocket for a fortnight and did not post it, which was quite uncharacteristic of him.

It is true that at times he gave voice to all the bitter feelings of disappointment and pain that welled up in him at what looked like the Church's rejection of the working classes. But he wanted such criticism to come *from within the Church*, as is proved by the fact that in May he broke off relations with an old friend, a Protestant pastor, who made use of the crisis to attack the Church. Henri even went so far as to cause one or two friends to break with the pastor, something very telling for a man to whom friendship was his very being.

It is true that he led an extremely solitary life, made no effort to contact any religious authority, and normally performed no religious duties. Yet he agreed to say Masses that

* The process of laicization puts a priest canonically into the situation of a baptized layman with his duties and rights in the Church. It does not obliterate the status of being a priest; it merely acquits him of the functions and duties, rights and privileges, of priestly status. In some cases it may be the outcome of canonical punishment. It may, on the other hand, be the answer given by religious authority to the demand made by a priest and backed up by serious motives.

he could have avoided—at Villecresnes on August 15, at the house of some friends in September, and at his family home in October. And on this last visit he took more trouble than ever before about the religious training of his little nephews and nieces.

But these facts are a mere fragment of truth, slight and incomplete, and no one (except God) can sort out the meaning and turn what is uncertain into certainty. His personal diary, which he had taken up again in 1951 and which he intended to go to his mother at his death, was destroyed by one of his friends who was ignorant of his intention (which might have changed anyway).

This book does not attempt to be a history of the priest-workers and their crisis. It is simply an attempt to trace the life of one of them.

Only one question seems to us permissible, and this we ask with calm consideration; to refrain from asking it might be one more instance of unnecessary prudence and, basically, of a lack of filial spirit and faith in the Church:

How was it that a priest of the Church, who had received so much from the Church, who had so many natural and spiritual gifts, and who had had a long spiritual and intellectual formation,

was led by the deepest impulse of his priesthood, devoted to the poorest and most neglected men and women of his time,

to consider, in deepest distress, and in order to be faithful to the Church, which is Christ, and at the same time to the poor, who are also Christ,

renouncing that very thing which, from the age of twelve, through twenty-five years of work, discovery, and hard-won victories, was the very heart of his life and fabric of his being:

his priesthood, his unique vocation to bring together his brothers and his God—that is to say, two worlds unknown to each other, the Church and the working class?

The real drama is that such a question should have to be asked at all.

DATE DUE

GAYLORD			PRINTED IN U.S.A.